THE

EVERYTHING KIDS'® Baseball BOOK

6TH EDITION

From baseball history to player stats—with
lots of homerun fun in between!

Greg Jacobs

Reporter/Statistician, STATS, LLC

Aadamsmedia

Avon, Massachusetts

PUBLISHER Karen Cooper

DIRECTOR OF ACQUISITIONS AND INNOVATION Paula Munier

MANAGING EDITOR, EVERYTHING® SERIES Lisa Laing

COPY CHIEF Casey Ebert

ACQUISITIONS EDITOR Katrina Schroeder

ASSOCIATE DEVELOPMENT EDITOR Elizabeth Kassab

SENIOR DEVELOPMENT EDITOR Brett Palana-Shanahan

EDITORIAL ASSISTANT Hillary Thompson

EVERYTHING® SERIES COVER DESIGNER Erin Alexander

LAYOUT DESIGNERS Colleen Cunningham, Elisabeth Lariviere, Ashley Vierra, Denise Wallace

An Everything® Series Book.
Everything® and everything.com® are registered trademarks of F+W Media, Inc.

Published by Adams Media, a division of F+W Media, Inc.
57 Littlefield Street, Avon, MA 02322. U.S.A.
www.adamsmedia.com

ISBN-10: 1-60550-641-9
ISBN-13: 978-1-60550-641-8

Printed by RR Donnelley, Owensville, MO, US

10 9 8 7 6 5 4 3 2

January 2011

This publication is designed to provide accurate and authoritative information with regard to
the subject matter covered. It is sold with the understanding that the publisher is not engaged
in rendering legal, accounting, or other professional advice. If legal advice or other expert
assistance is required, the services of a competent professional person should be sought.
—From a *Declaration of Principles* jointly adopted by a Committee of the
American Bar Association and a Committee of Publishers and Associations

Many of the designations used by manufacturers and sellers to distinguish their products are
claimed as trademarks. When those designations appear in this book and Adams Media was
aware of a trademark claim, the designations have been printed with initial capital letters.

Interior illustrations by Kurt Dolber.
Puzzles by Beth L. Blair.

This book is available at quantity discounts for bulk purchases.
For information, please call 1-800-289-0963.

Visit the entire Everything® series at *www.everything.com*

Contents

To Milo Cebu,
who loves his Cardinals

I would like to thank Dr. Fred Jordan for his close reading of several chapters. And, of course, thanks to my wife and sidekick Burrito Girl, who puts up with me when I write about sports.

Introduction

I have loved baseball all my life. Some of my earliest memories are of rooting for the Los Angeles Dodgers against the New York Yankees in the 1977 World Series. I can still remember that great Dodger infield of Steve Garvey at first base, Davey Lopes at second base, Bill Russell at shortstop, and "The Penguin" Ron Cey at third base.

Of this set of my then-favorite players, none made the Hall of Fame. None was the best ever at his position. In fact, I used to get into shouting matches about whether any of these folks was even the best player in 1977.

But even if these players weren't special to anyone else, they were special to me, because I rooted for them when I was a kid. Now, with an extra thirty years or so of perspective, I don't get upset when someone makes fun of Steve Garvey. Instead, I get upset when people don't recognize Johnny Bench as the greatest catcher in history.

The point is, I *care* about baseball. Other adults I know also take the game far more seriously than grown folks probably should. We watch major-league games; we talk about the games; we complain about the players; we stay up past 1 A.M. to see the Red Sox beat the Yankees (or vice versa). Why? Because we fell in love with the game when we were your age.

Since your parents were young, major-league baseball has evolved into new stadiums, with new league rules, new teams, and certainly different players. But the links to the past are always present. Maybe your mom's favorite player from when she was a girl is now managing somewhere. Perhaps you could go to a game at Wrigley Field in Chicago, where the Cubs have played since 1914—maybe your great-great-grandfather once attended a game there! Or you could listen to a Dodgers radio broadcast to hear broadcaster Vin Scully, who has been the voice of the Dodgers for fifty years.

The Everything® KIDS' Baseball Book, 6th Edition can be your guide to baseball past and baseball present. It's certainly fun to read straight through; but it can also be a useful reference. Are your grandparents always talking about the 1976 World Series? Read about what they saw in this book. Is your brother always staring at the box scores in the newspaper or online? Use this book to find out what those columns of numbers mean. Do you want to become a better player? This book gives you some ideas for developing your playing skills. Having trouble understanding your dad's fantasy baseball team? This book explains fantasy baseball, so you'll be able to give *him* pointers.

There's undoubtedly more to baseball than merely what is contained in this book. Appendix B, or your parents or a librarian, can suggest where to go to find more detail than what is included here. My simple hope is that by reading this book you can start to fall in love with baseball, just like I did years ago.

Chapter 1
Playing the Game

Baseball is a great game, one that is played and enjoyed by tens of millions of people. Many of those who appreciate the game grew up playing and watching baseball. Few get good enough to be a major leaguer, but everyone can learn how to play, and everyone can, with practice, become a better player. This chapter covers the fundamentals of baseball: the rules, the necessary skills, the positions of the players, and some ways to play baseball even if you don't have two teams of nine players available.

Rules of the Game

Baseball, at its heart, is a very simple game. A batter hits the ball, then tries to make it to first base (or farther!) without getting called out. Someone who gets all the way around the bases scores a run; whichever team scores the most runs during the game wins.

Teams take turns at bat. A team keeps batting until they make three outs; then they pitch to the other team until *they* make three outs. After each team has had nine turns, the game is over.

Here are the most common ways for the batter to make an out:

- **Strikeout.** A batter gets a strike if he swings and misses, or if he doesn't swing at a good pitch. Three strikes and the batter is out.
- **Flyout.** If a fielder catches a batted ball before it hits the ground, the batter is out.
- **Groundout.** If a fielder throws the ball to first base before the batter gets there, the batter is out.
- **Tagged out.** If a runner is not touching a base and is tagged with the ball, the runner is out.

inning: A turn at bat for each team is called an inning. A professional or college baseball game lasts for nine innings. High school and little league games are usually shorter—five, six, or seven innings.

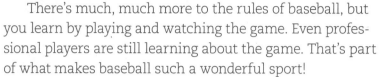
There's much, much more to the rules of baseball, but you learn by playing and watching the game. Even professional players are still learning about the game. That's part of what makes baseball such a wonderful sport!

Developing Your Baseball Skills

How can you develop your baseball skills? The answer is simple: play. Play a lot. Play with your friends, play in a league or two, play in the backyard with your family. The more you play, the more you'll learn about the game. You'll develop baseball instincts—you'll know what to do on the bases or in the field without even thinking about it. Your skills will get better and better. And whether or not you become a great player, you will likely develop a deep appreciation for the game of baseball that you can share with your friends and family. Many adults' most profound memories are of playing and watching baseball when they were kids your age.

For professional baseball you need two teams of nine players, each with uniforms and gloves, several brand-new baseballs, and some umpires . . . but all you *really* need to play a game is a few friends, an old tennis ball, and a stick for a bat.

Hitting

To become a good hitter, you have to hit—a lot. Of course you'll get to hit in games, but if you want to get more hitting practice, try these ideas:

- **Take a bucket of balls out to an empty field.** Have a friend pitch them all to you. Pick up all the balls and then you pitch them all to your friend.
- **Get some whiffle balls.** Whiffle balls are plastic balls with holes in them. Since they won't go far, they are

umpire: Umpires referee baseball games. They decide all close calls. Is the pitch a ball or a strike? Is the runner safe or out? Is the ball fair or foul? The umpire's decision is final. A good umpire can make a game much more fun: since the ump makes all the close decisions, instead of arguing with the other team, you can spend your time playing the game.

less likely to hurt someone or something. Whiffle balls are good for playing on a small field or in the backyard.

- **Hit balls off of a tee.** You can practice hitting the ball in different directions: try hitting ten balls to left field, then ten to center field, then ten to right field.
- **Go to a batting cage.** A machine will pitch a ball to you, and you can decide how fast you want the ball to come toward you.

Hitting Practice Is the Time to Experiment

Try out different kinds of bats—heavy bats, light bats, long bats, short bats, wooden bats, and metal bats. You don't necessarily have to buy yourself a brand-new bat to try it out. Ask to borrow a bat from a friend, or buy a cheap used bat at a secondhand store.

Then try different ways to stand. Mimic your favorite player's stance. Try out some of the advice a coach or a friend gave you. Find out what feels the most comfortable. As long as you can see the ball well, as long as you can "keep your eye on the ball" when you make contact, then your stance is fine. You may fine-tune it someday, but for now, go with what feels the best.

Most importantly, work on making contact with the ball. Don't worry about how hard you hit it—don't swing hard to hit home runs—just practice *hitting* the ball with every swing. After all this hitting practice, you'll find your hitting in games to be more consistent. Your body will know exactly what to do. You'll end up getting on base a lot. Eventually, without even trying, you'll start hitting the ball harder.

FUN FACT

What Is a Slump?

A slump is when a hitter stops getting hits for a while. Slumps happen to all hitters, even the best. Usually a slump lasts for only a few games, but sometimes it will go on for weeks. Hitters will try everything from extra batting practice to good luck charms to get out of a slump. When you hit a slump, just relax and try not to get too frustrated—all slumps have to end sometime.

Defense

The team that isn't batting is called the defense. Their job is to field the ball and put the batters out. The nine players on defense play the different positions described in the following list. Each position requires slightly different skills, though all defensive players must be able to throw well.

- **Infielders.** Those who play first base, second base, third base, and shortstop are called infielders. Infielders play close to the batter and to the bases. They field ground balls and try to throw out the batter. When a ball is hit into the outfield, the infielders receive the ball from the outfielders and try to tag out runners.
- **Outfielders.** The right fielder, left fielder, and center fielder are the outfielders. They play far away from the batter and the bases. Their main job is to catch fly balls and to throw the ball back to the infielders.
- **Catcher.** The catcher crouches behind home plate to catch any pitches that the batter doesn't hit. If a runner tries to steal a base, the catcher tries to throw the runner out.
- **Pitcher.** The pitcher starts all the action on the field by throwing every pitch to the batter. Pitchers also have to field ground balls and help out the infielders.

The best way to improve your baseball skills is to play in lots of games. A fielder needs to develop a "baseball sense" in addition to physical skills. This means not just being able to field and throw the ball, but knowing *where* to throw the ball and where to be on the field. When you're in the field, think to yourself before every pitch: If the ball comes to me, what do I do with it? If the ball doesn't come to me, where am I supposed to go? By answering these questions before every

WORDS to KNOW

choking up: Sometimes a coach will suggest that you choke up on the bat. This means to hold your hands higher above the end of the bat, as you can see in the picture. Choking up makes it easier to contact the ball, but more difficult to hit the ball hard.

WORDS to KNOW

ghost runner: You can play baseball with as few as two or three players per team. But let's say that a three-player team loads the bases. The next batter is standing on third base! What do you do? You put a "ghost runner" on third. The other runners run the bases as normal, but everyone pretends that the ghost runner is running too. You should make rules ahead of time about how to put a ghost runner out!

pitch in every game you play, you will build up good baseball instincts that you may not even be aware of. You'll find yourself making great plays simply because you knew what to do before the batter even hit the ball.

Throwing

The most important defensive skill, regardless of position, is throwing. Everyone on the field needs to be able to throw accurately over short and long distances.

How do you get good at throwing? Practice. Find a friend, grab your gloves, and play catch. Don't throw as hard or as fast as you can; just stand at a comfortable distance and practice throwing the ball right to your friend. For example, see how many throws you can make to each other without dropping the ball. Once you can make thirty or forty throws in a row, each of you take a big step back and try again.

If you want to practice throwing by yourself, find a heavy, solid wall, like the backboard at a tennis or handball court. Use chalk to lightly mark a square about chest high. Using a tennis ball, try to hit the wall inside the square. You can design a game—call a "strike" if the ball hits inside the square, call a "ball" if the ball hits on the line or outside the square. Try to earn a strikeout by throwing three strikes before you throw four balls. Once strikeouts become easy, take a step back and try again, or redraw a smaller square.

Fielding Ground Balls

When the batter hits a ground ball, the infielders try to pick up the ball, then throw to first base quickly to put the batter out. When you are developing your skill at fielding ground balls, don't worry about making the throw to first base. Start by making sure you can catch the ball every time.

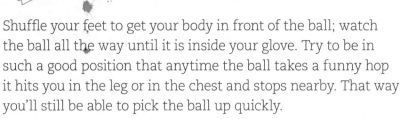

Shuffle your feet to get your body in front of the ball; watch the ball all the way until it is inside your glove. Try to be in such a good position that anytime the ball takes a funny hop it hits you in the leg or in the chest and stops nearby. That way you'll still be able to pick the ball up quickly.

The way to get good at fielding grounders is (surprise!) to practice. Set up some bases with a couple of friends. Put one person at bat, one person at first base, and one person at shortstop. Have the batter hit ground balls toward the short-stop, who should field them and throw to first base. Keep this up until the shortstop successfully fields five or ten balls in a row; then rotate who gets to play shortstop. Two friends can also roll grounders to each other. You can even practice grounders by throwing a tennis ball against a wall, and field-ing the rebound.

Catching Fly Balls

Outfielders especially have to practice fielding fly balls. The hardest part of catching flies is figuring out where the ball is headed. Once you know where the ball is going to land, run to that spot, turn toward the ball with your glove above your head, and catch the ball in front of you.

Try not to have to catch a ball while you're still running—this makes it harder to judge where the ball is, so it's more likely you'll drop it; also, if you're running, it will be harder to make the throw back to the infield. Of course, sometimes a ball is hit so far away from you that the only way to catch it is to keep running as hard as you can the whole way. But if you can manage to stop before you catch the ball, do it.

Fly ball practice is best done with a real batter, not just with someone throwing the ball in the air. Try to get friends to hit fly balls to you, especially if you have some friends who are good batters. High school kids or adults can give the best fly

FUN FACT

Even Major Leaguers Practice

One time, the great San Diego hitter Tony Gwynn didn't get a hit in a game that lasted almost until midnight. According to baseball lore, on his way home, Gwynn stopped by his old high school, where he had a key to the batting cage. He prac-ticed hitting in the cage for about an hour before he went to bed.

WORDS to KNOW

pull hitter: A right-handed pull hitter tends to hit the ball to left field every time. (Of course, a left-handed pull hitter tends to hit to right field.) Pull hitters usually generate a lot of power, but they are easy to defend against. The best hitters can also hit to the opposite field—in other words, a right-handed hitter will be able to hit toward right field.

FUN FACT

Little League Facts

Little League baseball began in 1939 in Williamsport, Pennsylvania, where the Little League World Series is still played today. Little League baseball is popular with boys and girls of all ages, from all over the world. Teams usually have between twelve and twenty players on them, and everyone on a team should get a chance to play.

Cobb on Hitting

Ty Cobb was one of the best hitters ever. He recommended that hitters not hold the bat all the way at the bottom. He suggested holding the hands an inch from the knob and keeping the hands an inch apart from each other for better balance and bat control. Not everyone should hit this way, but Ty Cobb had a career .367 batting average and made the Hall of Fame, so his advice might work!

ball practice, because they might have better bat control to hit a lot of good fly balls.

Pitching

In the major leagues, pitchers are specialists—that is, their job is only to pitch, and they rarely work on any other skills or play any other positions. Major-league pitchers spend their practice time building arm and leg strength, practicing different types of pitches, and resting their arms.

When younger people play baseball, however, the pitcher is just a good player who can throw the ball accurately. Pitchers who aren't pitching usually play elsewhere in the field. It is far, far more important for a pitcher to be able to hit a target than for a pitcher to throw hard, or to throw different pitches.

Professional pitchers throw 80, 90, or even 100 miles per hour; they throw curveballs, knuckleballs, sliders, and forkballs. But they are *professionals*. They are pitching to the best hitters in the world, so they must take every advantage they can find.

The best youth league and even high school pitchers don't necessarily throw hard or curvy stuff. They throw a fastball consistently to the catcher's glove every time, whether the catcher asks for a pitch inside or outside, high or low.

What kind of pitch can you throw besides a fastball? Try a changeup. You normally grip a fastball with your thumb and your first two fingers. Instead, try holding the ball all the way back in your palm, but use the same motion as you do for a fastball. You should find that this pitch goes just a bit slower; that's a changeup. Changeups are hard to hit because they throw off the batter's timing—the batter will be starting to swing just before the ball gets to the plate. If you can throw just a fastball and changeup, and if you can throw them right

Why do hitters like night baseball?

Connect the dots to find the answer to the above riddle.

Because there are more

to choose from!

to the catcher's glove on every pitch, then you will be an outstanding young pitcher.

Baseball Fun Without a Full Team

If you're short on players or equipment but you really want to play a game of baseball, don't panic! There are a few alternatives that are similar to baseball that you can play when you only have a few friends available or you can't get your hands on a bat, ball, or glove.

Punchball

This game uses the same basic idea of baseball, but if you don't have gloves, bats, or a field handy, you can use a tennis ball, or even a heavy wad of taped-up paper. Throw the ball up above your head, then swing your extended arm like a bat and "punch" the ball. Position as many fielders as you have at bases and in the outfield. You don't need a pitcher or a catcher, and if you don't have enough people to fill the other positions, you can shrink the field and only play with three bases and two outfielders (it's hard to punch a ball in to the outfield, anyway). Punchball is a good alternative to baseball or softball if you're looking for a baseball-like game to play with friends.

Two-Ball

This is a good baseball game for six to eight players. Divide the players into teams of two. Each pair takes a turn at bat while everyone else plays in the field. A pitcher pitches to a batter as in normal baseball. The batter hits the ball and runs to first . . . but the batter is out if any fielder can touch the ball before the batter reaches first base. Then the batter's partner bats.

Batting Cage Game

When you go to a batting cage, you usually get ten swings for a certain amount of money. You and a friend can have a friendly game of batting-cage baseball. Here's how it works: Every time you make contact, you get one point, even if you hit a foul ball. Every time you hit the ball beyond the pitching machine, you get two points. Every time you miss the ball, you lose one point. This game helps you concentrate on making contact with the ball. As you make contact more and more, you'll feel comfortable taking bigger swings to get more two-pointers; but you may also miss and lose some points.

Curve Ball

The curve ball is one of the trickiest pitches to hit. See if you can score by running a line of color through each of the curvy baseball terms in the following list! Instead of reading in a straight line, each word has <u>one</u> bend in it. Words can go in any direction.

HINT: One word has been done for you.

ASTROTURF

~~BLEACHERS~~

DUGOUT

HOMERUN

HOTDOG

POP FLY

SCOREBOARD

SHORTSTOP

STADIUM

WORLD SERIES

```
F L Y L E B O A R D T O
U P O R R L E R N P O P
G R O M F E S E I R E S
A C U P D A T S C T M D
S S T G I C O S H I R L
T K R U U H N D S N R
R B O E M O R E P U T O
I O U S R H O T R S G W
H O T T S T O P E S O O
O M D U U H O T M T U B
T D O L R K M M O A T L
R O G D B F E O H D M A
```

Catching with Style?

Some major leaguers make fancy catches on easy plays—Dave Parker of the Pirates and Reds used to flip his glove down for a "snap catch;" Andruw Jones of the Rangers sometimes catches the ball off to the side at hip level. Any coach will tell you that making a fancy catch in a game is a *bad idea*—what if you drop the ball?!?

The batting pair doesn't run the bases: base runners are ghost runners who advance whenever the batter gets a hit. After the batters make three outs, they go into the field, and the next pair comes in to bat. This is a fun but exhausting game. On offense, it will help you develop your ability to hit the ball where you want it to go; defenders will develop their range. Oh, and playing this game will help make sure you're in shape!

Off the Wall

This is a fun game you can play with two people, a ball, a glove, and a wall. You don't even need a glove if you're using a softer ball like a tennis ball.

Find a wall without windows where it's appropriate to throw a ball. You can use a vacant racquetball court, one wall of a gymnasium, or even the side of a barn. Next to the wall, mark off a territory to designate what is fair and what is foul. Use an area big enough that you can run from one end to the other in not too many steps. (Experiment to get the size right.)

To play, one player throws the ball high off the wall and the other person has to catch it. If the catcher catches the ball without it bouncing on the ground, he or she gets an "out." If the catcher drops it, the person throwing the ball has a runner on first base. If the ball bounces once before being caught, it's a single; twice, it's a double; three times, it's a triple; and four times, it's a home run. Always remember where your runners are, and keep track of how many runs you each score. Don't choose a space too big, or you'll never be able to cover the ground. Also, make a rule against throwing the ball so close to the wall that the only way to catch it is by crashing into the wall. Off the Wall is a good way to practice covering ground in the outfield and catching fly balls.

Chapter 2
The History of Baseball

T here are 30 major-league teams today, and many more minor league teams with players hoping to make it to the big leagues. There are thousands of college teams, high school teams, and little league teams all playing baseball. But where did it all begin? How did the major leagues get started? This chapter will answer all your questions!

The Earliest Games

Baseball has been played for well over 150 years. The game became well known around the United States during and after the Civil War, in the 1860s. Back then, pitchers threw underhanded, no one had gloves, the ball was softer than what we know as a baseball today, and the bases were 42 paces (probably about 120 feet) from each other—but it was baseball. The idea was to hit the ball, get from base to base safely, and score runs before getting three outs in your team's turn at bat.

Amateur teams were formed, and they played until the first team scored twenty-one runs, which at that time only took a few innings. In 1857 the idea of playing a nine-inning game was introduced, the bases were placed 90 feet apart, and more rules were changed.

The First Professional Teams

As far back as the 1860s there were barnstorming teams, which were teams that went from city to city playing each other. The first of these teams to be made up entirely of paid players was the Cincinnati Red Stockings of 1869. That first professional team's record was 57–0. In

FUN FACT

Vintage Base Ball

You can still watch Base Ball (as it was called in the mid-1800s) in its vintage form. The Elizabeth Resolutes, based in Elizabeth, New Jersey, play about thirteen games a year in which they dress in authentic 1800s uniforms and play by 1800s rules.

1871 the National Association of Professional Baseball Players was formed with nine teams. The Philadelphia Athletics were the first champions, winning 22 and losing only seven. By 1875 too much gambling caused people to lose interest in this league, but not in baseball. In 1876 the National League was formed. Many players from the original association became part of this new league, including "Cap" Anson, who was considered one of the game's first star players.

Through the 1880s and 1890s, several other leagues, including the American Association, the Players League, and a minor league called the Western League, began. All except the Western League failed.

Baseball Through the Decades

The modern era of baseball is said to have begun in 1900. Here is a look at what happened in baseball history in each of the decades of the 1900s and in the current century.

1900–1909

World Championships: Cubs 2, Boston Americans, New York Giants, White Sox, Pirates

Most famous players: Honus Wagner, Nap Lajoie, Ty Cobb, Cy Young, Christy Mathewson

In 1901 the Western League turned into the American League and started taking players from the National League. National League team owners were none too happy about this. The unfriendliness between the two leagues lasted for two years, until they finally united in 1903 and came up with the idea of a World Series between the two leagues.

FUN FACT

The Curse of the Bambino

Between 1903 and 1918, the Boston Red Sox won the World Series five times. Following the 1919 season, the Red Sox traded Babe Ruth ("the Bambino") to the New York Yankees. After the trade, the Red Sox didn't win another World Series for 86 years. They lost in the deciding game of the playoffs or World Series on six occasions. This misfortune is called the "Curse of the Bambino."

The Box Score

In the 1850s, New York newspaper writer Henry Chadwick invented a clever way of summarizing the results of a baseball game. His invention, the box score, lists the game's players and what they did in their at bats or on the pitching mound. The box scores you read today are quite similar to the ones Henry Chadwick put together. You can learn how to read a box score in Chapter 8.

The first decade of the 1900s featured a great Chicago Cubs team that won 116 games and lost only 36 in 1906. They played in three World Series and won two of them. The Cubs featured an incredible infield combination that included Joe Tinker at shortstop, John Evers at second base, and Frank Chance at first base.

Nap Lajoie was the American League's first batting champion, with an incredible .422 batting average, topped only once ever since. Ty Cobb and Honus Wagner were great hitters and had tremendous speed, stealing plenty of bases. Pitching was very different then: there were only five or six pitchers on a team, and starters pitched more often and for more innings than they do today. Hitters hit plenty of singles, doubles, and even triples, but home runs were not common, and league leaders did not top 16 homers through 1910.

1910–1919

World Championships: Red Sox 4, Philadelphia A's 3, Boston Braves, White Sox, Reds

Most famous players: Ty Cobb, Tris Speaker, Gavvy Cravath, Walter Johnson, Joe Jackson

The United States was immersed in the First World War during the latter part of this decade. Yet baseball continued uninterrupted. The major leagues were challenged by a new league called the Federal League, which spent a couple of years taking players away from the American and National Leagues. Finally the major leagues were able to reach an agreement with this new league, which was dissolved. John McGraw, one of baseball's all-time great managers, led the NL's New York Giants to four World Series, but no championships. In the American League, the Philadelphia Athletics,

led by their great manager Connie Mack, and the Boston Red Sox were the toughest teams.

Walter Johnson won 20 or more games every year in this decade. He was truly a great pitcher. But pitching was certainly easier back in this "dead-ball era." Until about 1920, the ball was much squishier than the baseballs we play with today, and the same ball was usually used for the entire game. Gavvy Cravath of the Philadelphia Phillies led the National League in home runs six times—but he never hit more than 24 homers in a season.

1920–1929

World Championships: Yankees 3, New York Giants 2, Indians, Washington Senators, Pirates, Cardinals, Philadelphia A's

Most famous players: Rogers Hornsby, Babe Ruth, Lou Gehrig, Lefty Grove, Grover Alexander

After World War I, the country entered a period called the Roaring Twenties, filled with plenty of singing, dancing, and great baseball. The Yankees began their 40-year

FUN FACT

Black Sox

In 1919 the Chicago White Sox earned the name "Black Sox." Eight players on the team were accused of being paid by gamblers to intentionally lose the series to the Reds. The first commissioner of baseball banned the eight players from the game forever. One of those players, "Shoeless" Joe Jackson, was one of baseball's all-time greatest hitters, but because he was kicked out of baseball, Jackson is not eligible for election to the Hall of Fame.

FUN FACT

Who Says Baseball Is a Slow Game?

World Series games in the first decade of the 1900s usually took about an hour and a half. That's amazing, considering that even regular season games today take close to three hours to play.

domination of the major leagues, during which they won 29 American League pennants and 20 world championships.

The dead-ball era was over in the 1920s. Though many sluggers emerged, it was Babe Ruth who captured the imagination of the fans. His record of 60 homers in 1927 stood for 34 years; his 714 career home runs were the most ever until 1974. "The Babe" was a big hero everywhere he went and was the first player to make as much as $50,000, which in those days was a very high salary—equivalent to at least half a million dollars in today's money. Whether it was because of all the home runs or not, baseball reached enormous popularity in the 1920s. In 1928, 61,000 people came to Yankee Stadium to watch the Yankees defeat the Cardinals

Stealing Bases

These teams are some of the first baseball teams in this country! Some are still around, while some have moved to different cities and changed their names. See if you can finish the teams' names by adding the missing letters **B-A-S-E-S.**

```
_ _ L T I M O R _  O R I O L _ _
_ O _ T O N  R _ D  _ O X
N _ W  Y O R K  M _ T _
_ R O O K L Y N  D O D G _ R _
L O _  _ N G _ L E _  _ N G _ L _
_ T L _ N T _  _ R _ V E _
```

in Game 1 of the World Series; nearly 40,000 attended Game 3 in the much smaller city of St. Louis. Baseball cemented its title as the national pastime.

1930–1939

World Championships: Yankees 5, Cardinals 2, Philadelphia A's, New York Giants, Tigers

Most famous players: Lefty Grove, Lou Gehrig, Johnny Mize, Jimmie Foxx, Hack Wilson, Dizzy Dean, Hank Greenburg

The Great Depression made the 1930s difficult for many Americans. Many people were out of work and money was scarce. Baseball was an escape from the tough times. Jimmie Foxx of the Philadelphia A's came close to Ruth's home run record, hitting 58 homers in one season. The Cubs' Hack Wilson set a one-season record that still holds today, driving in 191 runs. Babe Ruth played his last game for the Yankees in 1934, and then played a few with the Braves in 1935 before retiring. Ruth's teammate Lou Gehrig continued to play alongside a new teammate who appeared in 1936, another baseball legend named Joe DiMaggio. Gehrig retired because of a serious illness in 1937 after playing in 2,130 consecutive games, a record that many thought would never be broken.

Another lasting change to the game took place in 1935 in Cincinnati when the first night game was played. The idea

FUN FACT

Murderer's Row

The greatest lineup in baseball history is thought to be the 1927 lineup of the New York Yankees, nicknamed "Murderer's Row." Here are the season stats of some of their best players. As you look at these, remember that in 1927 only five players hit more than 20 home runs and that 100 RBIs has always been considered to be a very good season. These guys were incredible!

Position	Name	AVG	HR	RBI
1B	Lou Gehrig	.373	47	175
2B/3B/SS	Tony Lazzeri	.309	18	102
LF	Bob Meusel	.337	8	103
CF	Earle Combs	.356	6	64
RF	Babe Ruth	.356	60	164

Uniform Numbers

The Yankees were the first team to wear numbers on their backs in the 1920s. They started out by assigning numbers based on the batting order: Babe Ruth always hit third, so he was number 3. Lou Gehrig always hit fourth, so he was number 4, and so on. Today the number on a player's uniform is only used to identify the player, and has nothing to do with where the player bats.

FUN FACT

Retired Numbers

A team will sometimes "retire" the number of a famous player. This means that no one else on that team ever wears the retired number again—for example, the Cincinnati Reds retired Johnny Bench's number 5, so a Reds uniform with 5 on it will forever be associated with Bench. The Yankees have retired 16 different uniform numbers, the most of any team.

Travel by Train

Today, most teams get from one city to the other in a few hours by private jet. But through much of baseball's history, teams took trains on their road trips. That's the main reason why there were no major-league teams in the west or the south—a trip just from New York to Chicago meant sitting (and sleeping) on the train for an entire day.

caught on fast, and pretty soon many night games appeared on the schedule—except at Wrigley Field in Chicago, where night games were not played until 1988.

1940–1949

World Championships: Yankees 4, Cardinals 3, Reds, Tigers, Indians

Most famous players: Warren Spahn, Johnny Sain, Ted Williams, Joe DiMaggio, Bob Feller

World War II was the country's main focus in the first half of the 1940s, and many ballplayers left their teams to serve in the United States military. Young players and veterans who were too old for the military made up most of the teams. Since many of the men were in the army, women's baseball teams emerged, attracting a lot of attention as they played in their own league. The movie *A League of Their Own* is based on this 1940s women's baseball league.

Even though most young American people were off to war, baseball remained an important part of their lives. Soldiers were proud of their hometown teams, and they kept track of events in the major leagues as best they could. The infantrymen even used baseball questions to distinguish friend from foe. They say that General Omar Bradley once nearly failed to convince a lookout that he was an American soldier, because he didn't know that the Brooklyn Dodgers played in the National League.

Most soldiers returned from the war in 1945 and 1946, and the best athletes went into (or back into) major-league baseball. Ted Williams, Joe DiMaggio, and Bob Feller were among the most well known baseball and military heroes of the day. Williams in particular had already established himself as a great hitter, batting .406 in 1941. No one has batted

over .400 since then. Though he took three years off from baseball, Williams returned to the game in 1946 and batted over .300 every year until 1959.

Winning World War II required a full effort from all segments of American society. Afterward, many thought it ridiculous that black men were allowed to risk their lives in battle, but were (among other things) not allowed to play major-league baseball. Many great players, including Jackie Robinson, Cool Papa Bell, Josh Gibson, and Satchel Paige played in the Negro Leagues. There were many great players in these leagues, a number of whom would have been big stars in the major leagues if only the team owners would have let them play. In 1947, well before the civil rights movement of the 1960s, Brooklyn Dodgers general manager Branch Rickey promoted Jackie Robinson to the majors, thus breaking the "color barrier" and paving the way for the thorough integration of professional baseball over the next decades.

The Negro Leagues

The National League was formed in 1876, and in the early years of baseball people of any race could play. In fact, Moses Fleetwood joined the Toledo ball club in 1884 as the first black professional ballplayer, and others followed. But these players were treated badly by fans, opposing players, and their own teammates. Besides calling them names, white pitchers would often throw knockdown pitches at them. Little by little, there were fewer and fewer black players in baseball. There was no written rule, but owners no longer signed black players. Such informal—yet real—discrimination was typical in most parts of American society for a large part of the 20th century.

Since it was becoming impossible to get into the major leagues, black players (referred to in those days as Negroes)

Youngest Player Ever

In 1944, when most of the country's young men were involved in the war effort, 15-year-old Joe Nuxhall pitched in a game for the Cincinnati Reds to become the youngest major leaguer ever. Nuxhall was quickly sent back down to the minor leagues, but he rejoined the Reds in 1952 and played in the majors for 15 years.

Spahn and Sain

Warren Spahn and Johnny Sain led the pitching staff of the 1948 Boston Braves. Manager Billy Southworth wished he could let them pitch every day. So Gerald V. Hern of the *Boston Post* wrote a poem about them. The poem "Spahn and Sain and Pray for Rain" lives on in baseball's collective memory as a popular slogan for the '48 Braves.

Hard Ball

Baseball is a game full of action! Fill in as many wild words as you can, using the across and down clues. We left you some T-O-U-G-H letters and words as hints!

ACROSS

3. Fun baseball game played against an upright surface.

6. Team name: Pittsburgh

7. Nickname for a powerful hitter.

11. Smooth, round stick used to hit a baseball.

13. The 37 foot high wall in Boston's Fenway Park.

16. A "_____ hitter" is a hitter who hits for someone else.

17. To run from one base to another before the next player at bat has hit the ball.

19. Team name: San Francisco _____.

21. If the hitter bunts with a man on third base, it's called a "_____ play."

DOWN

1. Joe DiMaggio's nickname: "_____ 'n Joe."

2. When a hitter stops getting hits for a while.

4. Hank Aaron's nickname: "The _____."

5. "The _____" is when fans stand and then sit while moving their arms up and down in a motion that goes all around the stadium.

6. A "_____" fly goes high up in the air and is easily caught.

7. Sharp bumps on the bottom of baseball players' shoes.

8. "The Seventh Inning _____" gives fan a chance to get up and move around.

9. Team name: Los Angeles _____.

10. The score made by a player who touches first, second, third, and home base.

11. Jose Conseco and Mark McGwire were known as the "_____ Brothers."

12. A ball hit out of fair territory.

14. A _____ play is when a player is trapped between two bases. He has to scramble to get to one base or the other before being tagged out.

15. A "_____ ball" is the speediest pitch.

18. A player will sometimes have to _____ headfirst into a base to avoid being tagged out.

20. A "grand_____" is a home run hit when bases are loaded.

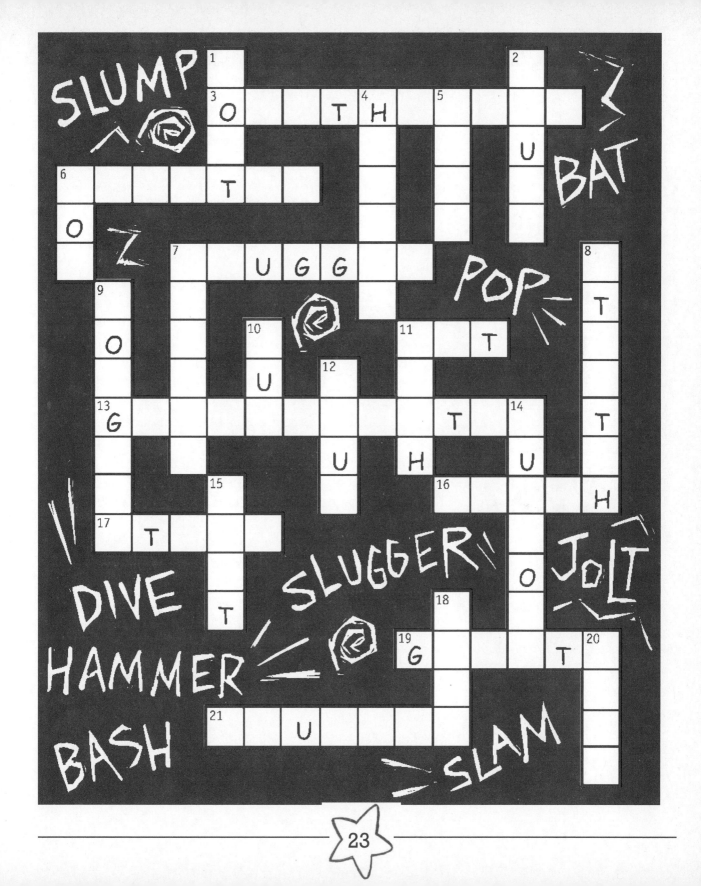

SLUMP

BAT

POP

DIVE

SLUGGER

JOLT

HAMMER

BASH

SLAM

23

Rookie of the Year

Since Jackie Robinson in 1947, the best first-year player in each league has been honored with the Rookie of the Year award.

FUN FACT

Why Brooklyn?

New York City consists of five large sections called boroughs. Unlike the Yankees and Giants, the Dodgers claimed to represent only one of these five boroughs, Brooklyn. But Brooklyn by itself was larger than any other American city except for Chicago!

began forming their own teams in the 1890s. By the early 1900s these teams were playing independently all over the eastern United States in cities like New York and Philadelphia. These teams often played exhibition games against major league teams, and they did well. It was obvious that many of the players on these teams had the talent to play in the major leagues, but the practice of discrimination was too strong.

Negro Leagues faced major problems, such as finding places to play. The teams often had to rent stadiums from white owners, who didn't always treat them fairly. Many owners did not allow them to use the "white" locker rooms. Nonetheless, the teams persisted, with players playing for the love of the game more than anything else, since most weren't making much money.

The Great Depression in the 1930s marked the end of the early Negro Leagues. Most of the teams, which had a hard time making money, had to call it quits. But touring teams such as the Pittsburgh Crawfords and Washington, D.C.'s Homestead Grays managed to play. Many major leaguers had great respect for the black ballplayers and still played exhibition games against these touring teams. By the late 1930s, as the country's economy improved, the Negro Leagues were back with new teams.

In the 1940s, Branch Rickey became determined to sign the first black major leaguer, despite the feelings of the other team owners. Rickey owned the Brooklyn Brown Bombers, a team in the Negro Leagues, and he was also the president and general manager of the Brooklyn Dodgers. In 1946, Rickey watched the Kansas City Monarchs come to town with a young player named Jackie Robinson. Rickey signed Robinson to a minor league contract in 1945, and called him up as a member of the Dodgers in 1947.

As more black players made the major leagues, there was less of a need for the Negro Leagues. While many of the greatest Negro League stars never made it to the major leagues, the leagues gave these ballplayers a place to show their great talents. It would eventually serve as a showcase for players to get to the major leagues. You can't help but wonder how some of the great major leaguers might have fared in daily competition against all of the country's best athletes, not just those who happened to be white.

1950–1959

World Championships: Yankees 6, New York Giants, Milwaukee Braves, Brooklyn Dodgers, Los Angeles Dodgers

Most famous players: Willie Mays, Mickey Mantle, Duke Snider, Ted Williams, Whitey Ford, Stan Musial

The city of New York dominated baseball. Their three teams—the Yankees, the Giants, and the Dodgers—were the best in the game, and they competed for the city's attention. One of the most memorable moments from those New York rivalries occurred at the end of the 1951 season. The New York Giants and the Brooklyn Dodgers were tied for first place in the NL, so they played one game to see which team would go to the World Series. The Dodgers led the game 4–1 going into the bottom of the ninth inning.

The Giants got one run to make the score 4–2, then Bobby Thompson came to bat against pitcher Ralph Branca with two men on base. Thompson hit a home run to left field, winning the game 5–4 and sending the Giants to the World Series. On the radio, Giants announcer Russ Hodges conveyed the fans' excitement with his famous call, shouting over and over,

Rube Foster

Rube Foster was one of the great pitchers of the early 1900s. He pitched for the 1906 Philadelphia Giants and went on to found the Negro Leagues, which debuted in 1920 with eight teams. In 1923, Foster helped start a second league with six new teams.

Paige on Age

Negro Leagues star and former major league pitcher Satchel Paige, who pitched for nearly 30 years and even appeared in a major league game at the age of 59, once said, "Age is a case of mind over matter. If you don't mind, it don't matter."

"The Giants win the pennant! The Giants win the pennant!" Thompson's home run became known as the "shot heard round the world."

In the 1950s, refrigerators, washing machines, and other new technologies began to change the way Americans lived. Two new technologies caused lasting changes in major league baseball. The first was the beginning of televised baseball. Though virtually every game can be seen on TV today, in the early 1950s most people didn't even own television sets. But by the end of the decade, millions of people could watch a baseball game even when they couldn't physically go to the game.

It might have been the jet airplane that ended the great New York baseball rivalries. By the end of the 1950s, travel by jet was common, meaning that people could get from the country's East Coast to the West Coast in less than a day. And, after World War II, the population of California grew very rapidly. To take advantage of the many potential new fans, both the Dodgers and the Giants moved to the West Coast in 1958—the Dodgers to Los Angeles, the Giants to San Francisco.

1960–1969

World Championships: Yankees 2, Dodgers 2, Cardinals 2, Pirates, Orioles, Tigers, Mets

Most famous players: Bob Gibson, Sandy Koufax, Don Drysdale, Hank Aaron, Frank Robinson, Willie McCovey, Carl Yastrzemski

New York maintained its reign as the focus of the baseball world, as the Yankees played in the World Series in 1960–1964. Yankee outfielder Roger Maris dueled with

teammate Mickey Mantle for the 1961 home run crown—Maris hit number 61 on the last day of the season, breaking Babe Ruth's hallowed record.

The 1960s were a time of expansion. The number of teams in each league hadn't changed for many decades. But in 1961, the American League added two new teams, the Los Angeles Angels and the Washington Senators. A year later, the National League added two new teams, the New York Mets and the Houston Colt 45s, who became the Astros. New teams are usually not very good, but in 1962 the Mets won only 40 games while losing 122 in the new 162-game season. This was the worst record ever, and the Mets were greeted with many appropriate jokes.

Baseball expanded by four more teams in 1969: the Montreal Expos and San Diego Padres in the National League, the Seattle Pilots (who became the Milwaukee Brewers after just one year) and Kansas City Royals in the American League. The twelve-team leagues were split into two six-team divisions, east and west.

Now you're probably wondering what happened to those terrible Mets. Well, after being pretty dreadful for seven years, they shocked the world in 1969. The same year that people landed on the moon for the first time ever, the Mets beat the Baltimore Orioles in five games to win the World Series.

1970–1979

World Championships: A's 3, Pirates 2, Reds 2, Yankees 2, Orioles

Most famous players: Reggie Jackson, Joe Morgan, Willie Stargell, Tom Seaver, Catfish Hunter, Pete Rose, Johnny Bench

WORDS to KNOW

pennant: The team that represents the National League or the American League in the World Series is said to have won the pennant.

FUN FACT

The Asterisk

When Babe Ruth hit his 60 homers in 1927, teams played 154 games in a season. But in 1961, the American League changed to a 162-game schedule—Roger Maris had eight extra games to beat the Babe's record! Commissioner Ford Frick decreed that Maris's record of 61 homers should be listed with an asterisk indicating the extra games that Maris played.

League Championship Series

Until 1969, whichever team won the most regular-season games in each league went to the World Series. But starting in 1969, the leagues were split into divisions. The League Championship Series, or LCS, was played between the division winners. So today, the ALCS and the NLCS decide which team in each league goes to the World Series.

Just 35 years ago, the major leagues were very different than they are today. For one thing, players could not be "free agents." Once a player was assigned to a team, he could not change teams unless he was traded or released. In 1972 the Major League Baseball players went on strike; they won the right to free agency a few years later.

Teams didn't usually score as many runs as they do today, and owners wanted to increase scoring. For example, in the American League in 1970, teams averaged 4.2 runs per game; in 2008, they averaged 4.6 runs per game. They had already lowered the height of the pitching mound in 1968, from fifteen inches to its current height of ten inches. So, in 1973 the American League introduced the "designated hitter."

Many teams moved into bigger stadiums in the 1970s, most of which used the same AstroTurf that the Astros put inside their dome. Turf caused the baseball to take high bounces, forcing fielders to adjust their positioning. Speed became a more important part of the game. In 1977 Lou Brock became the first player ever to steal 900 bases, breaking Ty Cobb's previous record of 892. (Rickey Henderson has since passed them both.) Most of these old stadiums were shaped like enormous concrete circles, and were also used for football games, concerts, rodeos, and other big events. Tickets were much cheaper then than now. In those days, a $5 ticket might be considered outrageously expensive; if a $5 ticket is available today, it's as a special discount.

On April 8, 1974, "Hammerin'" Hank Aaron of the Atlanta Braves hit his 715th career home run, one more than Babe Ruth hit. Aaron went on to finish his career where he began it, in Milwaukee, with 755 homers.

1980–1989

World Championships: Dodgers 2, Phillies, Cardinals, Orioles, Tigers, Royals, Mets, Twins, A's

Most famous players: Ozzie Smith, Nolan Ryan, Dennis Eckersley, Mike Schmidt, George Brett, Wade Boggs, Tony Gwynn, Ricky Henderson

Free agency caused player salaries to increase rapidly. In response, owners tried to limit players' abilities to change teams, and baseball players went on strike in the middle of the 1981 season. More than 700 games were canceled, and when baseball finally returned, the season was split into two halves. The winners of the first half played the winners of the second half in a special playoff series. Fans were not happy, and did not watch much baseball on television or at the park in the second part of the 1981 season.

Baseball recovered as the decade went on. Half of the twenty-six teams played in at least one World Series in the 1980s, and nine different teams won championships. Speed continued to be a critical element of strategy, as pitchers had a hard time preventing the stolen base. In 1981, Rickey Henderson, king of the stolen base, stole a record 130 bases in one season.

The art of base stealing peaked in the 1980s, but the art of relief pitching was only beginning. Until the 1970s it was normal for the starting pitcher to pitch the whole game. Relief pitchers, whose specific role was to pitch only the late innings, became much more specialized in the 1980s. Most teams began to use a "closer," a relief pitcher with the job of finishing just the last inning or two. Toward the end of the decade, teams began to use "setup" relievers, who relieved the starter in the seventh or eighth inning but gave way to the closer in the ninth.

Best Record, No Reward

The team with the best record in the 1981 season was the Cincinnati Reds. However, because of the strike and the split season, they didn't make it to the World Series; they didn't even make it to the playoffs. They finished second to the Dodgers in the first half and second to the Astros in the second half.

WORDS to KNOW

designated hitter: A designated hitter (DH) is a player who bats for the pitcher. The American League uses the DH, but the National League does not—NL pitchers must bat for themselves. Since pitchers aren't usually good at hitting, this means more runs are usually scored in AL games.

FUN FACT

Family Affair

At one time, Cal Ripken Jr. and his brother Billy both played for the Baltimore Orioles, with their dad as coach. In 1987 and 1988 their dad was also the manager.

1990–1999

World Championships: Yankees 3, Blue Jays 2, Reds, Twins, Braves, Marlins

Most famous players: Greg Maddux, Tom Glavine, John Smoltz, Randy Johnson, Cal Ripken Jr., Barry Bonds, Mark McGwire

The major leagues expanded even more in the 1990s with the addition of the Florida Marlins, Colorado Rockies, Arizona Diamondbacks, and Tampa Bay Devil Rays. This brought the number of major league teams to today's total of thirty. The playoff structure was changed once again in 1994, to the present format. Each league was split into three divisions—east, central, and west.

In 1995, Cal Ripken Jr. of the Orioles played in his 2,131st consecutive game, breaking the record Lou Gehrig set in 1939. The September 6 game drew a sellout crowd, which included the president of the United States, and millions of fans around the world watched on TV. Ripken ended his streak in 1998, after playing 2,632 consecutive games.

In one of the saddest episodes in baseball history, a strike ended the 1994 baseball season in August. It was the first time since 1904 that there was no postseason, no World Series, and no championship team. Millionaire players and millionaire team owners got very little sympathy from the fans, who were unhappy that they couldn't watch and enjoy their favorite game. When baseball returned in 1995, attendance was way down. For the next couple of seasons many fans were turned off to baseball.

In 1997 baseball owners decided that they'd try to draw fans back by starting interleague play, which meant regular season games between National and American league teams. Longtime baseball fans weren't happy

about it, but on June 12, 1997, the Texas Rangers and the San Francisco Giants played in the first interleague game. What at first appeared to be a novelty caught on as cross-town rivals like the Cubs and White Sox in Chicago, The A's and Giants in neighboring Oakland and San Francisco, and the Mets and Yankees in New York all faced each other during the season.

Starting in the mid-1990s, players hit more home runs than ever before. In 1983, Mike Schmidt hit 40 home runs to lead the league. But in 1996, 40 home runs was only good for twelfth best in the majors. In 1998, two players hit more home runs in the season than ever before. Sammy Sosa hit 66 and Mark McGwire hit 70, both breaking the single-season record of 61 Roger Maris had held since 1961.

There are several possible reasons for this offensive explosion. For one thing, players took weight training more seriously than ever before. In the 1980s, many teams did not even have their own weight rooms—players on the road had to find a local gym if they wanted to work out. But by the 1990s, teams built gyms, hired athletic trainers, and reaped the benefits of regular workouts. A second possible reason was the league's expansion. The addition of four new teams meant that more than forty pitchers who previously weren't good enough to play in the majors were now pitching to the world's best power hitters.

But in the early 2000s, it came to light that many players were using illegal drugs called anabolic steroids to build their muscles. Sluggers Ken Caminiti and Jose Canseco came forward to tell of their own steroid use and to warn that many others were also using the same drugs. No other players directly admitted to using steroids. However, Barry Bonds was investigated by the FBI and Mark McGwire and Sammy Sosa were called to testify before Congress about their own steroid use. It's still not clear exactly which

The Nasty Boys

The Reds of the 1990s used a combination of outstanding relief pitchers. Randy Myers, Rob Dibble, and Norm Charlton regularly held late-inning Reds leads. Two of these three "Nasty Boys," Dibble and Myers, were named most valuable player (MVP) of the 1990 NLCS.

WORDS to KNOW

wild card: The winner of each division earns a spot in the playoffs. But a fourth team in each league also makes the playoffs—the team that has the next-best record in the league after the division winners. This "wild card" team has the same chance to win the World Series as any other playoff team; in fact, four wild card teams have won the championship.

FUN FACT

The Minor Leagues

Each major league team supports several minor league teams, which played even through the strike of 1994. Almost every player spends a few years in the minors before coming to the major leagues. Some players are sent back down to the minor leagues if they are not playing well, and sometimes good major league players will go to the minors after an injury to get used to playing again. Minor league teams are in many smaller cities across the country.

players were using steroids. But in 2005, the major leagues instituted steroid testing for all players. Since then, players have been hitting fewer home runs than they did a decade ago.

2000–2009

World Championships: Red Sox 2, Yankees 2, Diamondbacks, Angels, Marlins, Cardinals, Phillies

Most famous players: Pedro Martinez, Roger Clemens, Johan Santana, Manny Ramirez, Albert Pujols, Randy Johnson, Ichiro Suzuki, Chipper Jones

The terrorist attacks of 2001 put a halt to baseball, but only for a week. The sport, and especially the Yankees' berth in the 2001 World Series, served as a rallying point for American culture. Since 2001, many teams have replaced the traditional singing of "Take Me Out to the Ball Game" during the seventh-inning stretch with "God Bless America."

The Chicago Cubs haven't won a World Series since 1908; the Boston Red Sox hadn't won since 1918. Both teams have been considered cursed for as long as most people can remember. In 2003, both teams were very good, and both seemed to have a good chance to make the World Series. But both faltered in the playoffs. The Cubs are still waiting for their championship, but the Red Sox earned their revenge in 2004. In the ALCS, they fell behind to the Yankees three games to none, but they came all the way back to win four games to three. Then they swept the St. Louis Cardinals to win their first World Series in 86 years.

Throughout the 2000s, the New York teams spent money like crazy trying to win. But they couldn't quite seem to beat teams with smaller payrolls. The decade began with a sub-

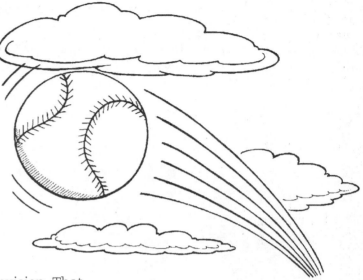

way series between the Yankees and Mets in 2000. The Yankees made the playoffs every year from 2000–2007 but couldn't win another championship until 2009; the Mets only even returned to the playoffs once, and they blew big division leads in both 2007 and 2008. In the 2000s, teams learned that spending money is less important than spending money wisely.

Perhaps the biggest change to the game in the new century is in its national exposure. When your parents were growing up, they could see the home team and one or two other games of the week on television. That was it. In the 1990s, cable television allowed people to watch a bit more baseball. But now it is possible to see every game every night on the Internet, or on satellite television. Every radio broadcast can be heard on the Internet, or on satellite radio. The Internet allows instant access to box scores and stories about every game. Fantasy baseball is growing in popularity, once again due to the Internet.

Even though the game continues to evolve, baseball is still fundamentally the same game that your parents and grandparents watched and played when they were your age. Ask them what stories they have about baseball history; they might be thrilled to tell you about the players and the teams they used to watch. And savor the games you watch now. Some day your own grandchildren might be asking you about your favorite baseball memories.

FUN FACT

Following a Game on the Internet

Several sites, including *www.mlb.com*, allow you to see the status of a game as it happens. Free applets show who's at bat, who's pitching, lineups, a live box score, and much more.

Say What?

Yogi Berra was known as being quite a talker behind the plate. He hoped his chatter would distract the batter! The story goes that in the 1958 World Series, with the legendary Hank Aaron hitting, Yogi kept telling Aaron to "hit with the label up on the bat." Finally, Aaron couldn't stand it any more. He turned to Yogi and said "_____!"

To find out what Hank Aaron said to Yogi Berra, figure out where to put each of the cut apart pieces of the grid.

C'mon Hank, hit it with the label up. Up, up, up, with the label up. C'mon Hank, hit it with the label up...

Chapter 3
The National League

Baseball today is played by all sorts of teams, organized into youth leagues, high school districts, college conferences, semi-pro leagues, and minor leagues. The best-known teams play in the major leagues: the National League and the American League. Some of these teams, like the Dodgers and Yankees, have been around since well before even your great-grandparents were born. Others are as few as ten years old. In this chapter, you can read about every National League team—including, perhaps, your favorite team.

The Start of the National League

In the 1870s, the National Association, one of the first-ever professional baseball leagues, was having trouble. The team owners weren't following the league rules. The Boston Red Stockings seemed to win all the time. There was some shady business with gamblers who might have been fixing games. William Hulbert, owner of the Chicago White Stockings, convinced seven other owners to join with him in a new league: the National League. Only two of the teams are still playing today.

The Original 1876 National League

1876 Team Name	Modern Team Name
Chicago White Stockings	Chicago Cubs
Philadelphia Athletics	The Philadelphia Athletics only played in the NL in 1876.
Boston Red Stockings	Atlanta Braves
Hartford Dark Blues	The Hartford Dark Blues only played in the NL in 1876 and 1877.
Mutual of New York	Mutual of New York only played in the NL in 1876.
St. Louis Brown Stockings	The St. Louis Brown Stockings only played in the NL in 1876 and 1877.
Cincinnati Red Stockings	The Cincinnati Red Stockings only played in the NL from 1876–1880.
Louisville Grays	The Louisville Grays only played in the NL in 1876 and 1877.

Teams joined and left the National League a lot, especially in its early years. Now, the league contains 16 teams.

Philadelphia Phillies

The Phillies won the World Series in 2008, in the same year they achieved something less memorable: they lost their 10,000th game in team history, the most ever for an American sports franchise. They sure had some bad years; at two points, they went more than a decade without a winning record. That all changed in the late 1970s, when managers Danny Ozark and then Dallas Green led the team to seven

division titles in nine winning seasons. In 1993, colorful characters John Kruk, Lenny Dykstra, Mitch Williams, and others took the team to the World Series.

From 1971–2003, the Phillies played in Veterans Stadium, a flying-saucer-style stadium with rock-hard artificial turf. They moved into a modern ballpark with a beautiful grass field in 2004. The move has coincided with recent success— the Phillies have managed a winning record every year from 2003–2009.

Philadelphia Phillies

Founded in 1883
Other names: Philadelphia Quakers, Philadelphia Blue Jays
2 World Championships (1980, 2008)
7 NL pennants

Famous Phillies: Mike Schmidt, 1972–1989

Many baseball fans consider Mike Schmidt to be the best all-around third baseman ever to play the game. He was a truly awesome power hitter, leading the league eight times in home runs. In just 17 years he placed himself among the top 10 all-time leaders in homers, won three MVPs, and helped lead the Phillies to their first ever World Championship. On the other side of the field, he was a tremendous defensive player. He won the Gold Glove as the best fielding third baseman in the National League nine times. He went about his business very seriously and fans and players alike respected and admired his talent and his work ethic. Schmidt retired in 1989 and was elected to the Hall of Fame in 1995.

Who was the most famous Phillie?

In this chapter, you'll read short notes about famous players on some teams. But since baseball has been around for such a long time, there are way more players than there is room to write about them. If you want to learn more about famous players on your favorite team, check out the *Baseball Encyclopedia*.

Mike Schmidt

HR	RBI	AVG
548	1,595	.267

Colorado Rockies

The Rockies were an unusual team from the beginning, simply because of where they play. Denver, Colorado, is known as the Mile High City because it is located more than 5,000 feet (about a mile) above sea level. Why is this important? At high altitudes, breaking balls don't curve very much, which makes them easier to hit, and batted balls fly farther. For the first nine years of the team's existence, Rockies home games were nearly always slugfests. From 1995–2001, Coors Field saw an average of 13.8 runs and 3.2 home runs *per game!* Since 2002, the Rockies have stored their baseballs in a specially made humidor that cost $15,000. The humidor controls temperature and humidity so the balls won't be damaged by Denver's low humidity.

Through their first decade, the Rockies focused on finding the best sluggers. The "Blake Street Bombers," led by Andres Galarraga, put the Rockies in the playoffs in 1995. More recently, the team has developed some excellent pitchers. They made their second playoff appearance ever in 2007 after winning 14 of their last 15 regular season games. They made it to the World Series but were swept by the Boston Red Sox for the championship. The Rockies returned to the playoffs in 2009, but they lost in the first round.

Boo!

Philadelphia is known as a tough town in which to be a sports star. The fans take pride in yelling "Boo!" all the time. In fact, even though Phillies fans worship Mike Schmidt as one of their town's best professional athletes ever, the Veteran's Stadium crowd once booed him. But that shouldn't make him feel too bad—Philadelphia fans famously booed Santa Claus at a football game!

Colorado Rockies

Founded in 1993
0 World Championships
1 NL pennant

St. Louis Cardinals

The Cardinals' 10 World Series victories put them second best in history, behind the Yankees, but they didn't start out as a good team. They were founded in 1882 as the St. Louis Brown Stockings, the name of a team that went bankrupt in 1877. It wasn't until the 1920s and the arrival of manager Branch Rickey that the Browns truly came into their own. They only had three losing seasons in the entire 1920s, 1930s, and 1940s put together, which led to nine playoff appearances. Outfielder Stan "the Man" Musial was their best player of this era, and his statue stands outside new Busch Stadium today.

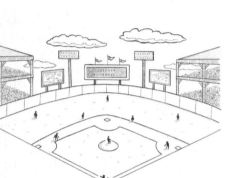

In the past 30 years, the Cardinals have been similarly successful, if not as spectacularly consistent. The "White Rat," Whitey Herzog, managed the team to three World Series appearances in the 1980s with a team designed for speed on the artificial turf of old Busch Stadium. In 1996, Tony La Russa took over as manager and has had the team to the playoffs in seven of his 13 years.

St. Louis Cardinals

Founded in 1882
Other names: St. Louis Brown Stockings, St. Louis Browns, St. Louis Perfectos
10 World Championships (1926, 1931, 1934, 1942, 1944, 1946, 1964, 1967, 1982, 2006)
17 NL pennants

Famous Cardinals: Ozzie Smith, 1978–1996

Just 28 homers in 19 years? How can a player with those kind of career numbers be one of the all-time best Cardinals? Ozzie Smith represents the other side of the game:

defense. He was called the "Wizard of Oz" because no one had ever played shortstop like Ozzie. He could get to ground-balls that no one else could reach, often diving in either direction before somehow making the throw to first base for the out. He also turned more double plays than any player in history.

Ozzie dazzled the fans and frustrated the opponents who thought they had a hit until he turned it into an out. He won a record 13 Gold Gloves and led the league nine times in fielding percentage at shortstop. When Ozzie came up he wasn't much of a hitter, but by the late 1980s he had established himself as a decent batter who drew plenty of walks. He could also steal bases, picking up 580 in his 19-year career—that's more than 30 per year. Smith was a team leader and a fan favorite. He retired in 1996 and joined the Hall of Fame in 2002.

Ozzie Smith

HR	RBI	AVG
28	793	.262

Houston Astros

In 1962, the National League added the Colt .45s and the New York Mets to expand to ten teams—the first time a major league had welcomed new teams since before 1900. The other National League owners were a bit worried about playing games in the incredibly hot and humid Texas summers, so the city of Houston built the first air-conditioned indoor stadium: the Astrodome.

Until the 1980s, the Astros weren't known for much beyond their stadium and their rainbow uniforms. However, fortunes changed, and they made the playoffs three times

WORDS to KNOW

Gold Glove: Each year the best fielder at each position in both the National and American Leagues is given the Gold Glove award for fielding excellence.

FUN FACT

Why Astros?

In the 1960s, when the Astrodome was built, the United States was engaged in a space race, one goal of which was to send people to the moon. The control center for the U.S. space program was located in Houston. The former mayor of Houston who owned the team named the new indoor stadium the Astrodome and renamed the team the Astros. When an artificial surface was installed in the Astrodome, fake grass quickly became known as AstroTurf.

in the 1980s. In 1986, the team looked World Series-bound behind the pitching of Mike Scott, whose no-hitter on September 25 clinched the division title. But in Game 6 of the National League Championship Series—a 16-inning marathon—the Mets snuffed a final Astros rally to advance.

In the 1990s, the Astros continued their winning ways. Since 1992 the Astros have had only three losing seasons, and they've shown up in the playoffs six times. Nevertheless, their first World Championship is still in the future.

Houston Astros

Founded in 1962
Other names: Houston Colt .45s
0 World Championships
1 NL pennant

Famous Astros: Craig Biggio, 1988–2007

Though he was an outstanding athlete in many sports, Craig Biggio chose to make baseball his career. He joined the Astros in 1988 as the rare catcher who could hit really well, and made the all-star team in 1991 as a catcher. However, in order to lengthen his career, Biggio moved to second base in 1992—and made the all-star team again.

Craig Biggio

HR	RBI	AVG
291	1,175	.281

Biggio has played in more games than any other Astro. At his last game in 2007, a sold-out crowd cheered him into

retirement. The Astros retired his number 7 the next year. Though he's from New York originally, twenty years of playing in Houston seem to have rubbed off on Biggio, who is now the head baseball coach of a Houston high school team.

Florida Marlins

Even though they've only been around since 1993, the Marlins already have won two World Series championships. For their first, in 1997, the team brought in many star players who earned big, big salaries. Even though they won, the team owner decided he couldn't afford to keep paying his stars. So the team held a fire sale, in which they traded pretty much every good player on the team. Thus, the Marlins were the worst team in baseball for the next two years and didn't have another winning season until 2003.

The good news was that the Marlins got talented players in trades and draft choices during their fire sale. In 2003, 72-year-old Jack McKeon took over as manager and led his young team to the playoffs, where they won close series against the Giants, the Cubs, and finally the Yankees in the World Series.

Since then, the Marlins have been known for having the smallest payroll in the majors—the entire Marlins team has usually made less money than one star player for the Yankees. But the Marlins have still managed to field good teams. They will try to continue their success as they move into a new stadium, which is planned for the 2012 season. When they move, they will change the team's name to the Miami Marlins.

Florida Marlins

Founded in 1993
2 World Championships (1997, 2003)
2 NL pennants

San Francisco Giants

Even though the Giants have played in San Francisco for all of your life and (probably) for all of your parents' lives, for many years they were known as the New York Giants. During that time their main rivals were the cross-town Dodgers. But in 1957, the Giants moved to California. There, they played for many years in Candlestick Park. In 2000, the Giants moved into Pac Bell Park, where home runs to right field can splash down into McCovey Cove.

The Giants last won the World Series in 1954, when they were still in New York. Since then, they've made it to the playoffs many times, and they've even been to the World Series three times. But they've always lost, often in crazy, unlucky ways. In the ninth inning of Game 7 in 1962, Willie McCovey hit a screaming line drive that could have driven in two runs to win the series—but the second baseman made a great catch to end the game. In 1993, the Giants won 103 games, but the Braves clinched the division on the last day of the season with 104 wins. In the 2002 World Series, the Giants were up 5–0 in the seventh inning of the game that would have won the series, but the Angels came back to win it. The next year, the Giants lost to the Marlins on the last play of the series when the tying run was thrown out at the plate to end the game. Aargh! Since 2003, the Giants have not made the playoffs, but they hope to contend soon behind 2008 Cy Young winner Tim Lincecum and a strong pitching staff.

The Cy Young Award: The Cy Young Award, named after the pitcher with the most wins in baseball history, is given each year to the best pitcher in each league.

Amazing Mays

A Giants broadcaster, in awe of one of Mays' hits, said "The only player who could have caught that ball, hit it."

San Francisco Giants

Founded in 1883
Other Names: New York Gothams, New York Giants
5 World Championships (1905, 1921, 1922, 1933, 1954)
17 NL pennants

Famous Giants: Willie Mays, 1951–1973

He was known as the "Say Hey Kid," and was one of the greatest and most likable players to ever play the game. After his rookie season in 1951, Mays spent two years in the army before returning to the (then New York) Giants, with whom he racked up 41 homers and won the World Championship over the Cleveland Indians. Willie could do it all. He hit for power, leading the league in homers four times, and he also had great speed, leading the league in stolen bases four times. He was known for incredible defense; with his basket catch, he used the glove as a "basket" to catch fly balls at his waist. Perhaps the most famous catch Mays ever made came in the first game of the 1954 World Series as he grabbed a ball going over his head in the deepest part of center field to help the Giants hold on and win. After many years with the Giants in San Francisco, Mays spent his last couple of years back in New York with the Mets before retiring as the third greatest home run hitter ever. A baseball legend, Mays made the Hall of Fame in 1979.

Willie Mays

HR	RBI	AVG
660	1,903	.302

FUN FACT

The Windiest Ballpark

Candlestick Park—the stadium where the 49ers football team still plays—was built in an unsheltered area right next to San Francisco Bay. Candlestick was known for being very windy and cold, even in the summer. Take a look at highlights of Giants games there and you'll see hot dog wrappers blowing all over the place and fans huddling under blankets. Once the wind blew a pitcher off the mound!

"He's Always There"

Former Dodger player and manager Gil Hodges talked about how good a defensive player Willie Mays really was. "I can't very well tell my hitters, don't hit it to him. Wherever they hit it, he's always there."

Arizona Diamondbacks

The Diamondbacks, the youngest National League team, started play barely more than a decade ago. In that time they've seen both highs and lows. The team brought in a number of star free agents, including fan favorite Luis Gonzalez, so they would be good right away. Sure enough, they made the playoffs in three of their first five seasons, and even won a dramatic World Series against the Yankees in 2001. Afterward, the D-backs had to get rid of many of these stars because they could no longer afford their salaries. So, for a few years they were really bad as they tried to rebuild. Still, the D-backs have managed a winning record in seven of their first 12 seasons. That's a success any team should be proud of.

The Diamondbacks play in a big, quirky ballpark in Phoenix, Arizona. The center field fence is tall and deep. The team has always put outstanding pitchers on the mound, taking advantage of the large field. Curt Shilling and Randy Johnson were co-MVPs of the 2001 World Series; today, 2003 Rookie of the Year and 2006 all-star Brandon Webb leads the D-backs pitching staff.

Arizona Diamondbacks

Founded in 1998
1 World Championship (2001)
1 NL pennant

The Big Unit Is Scary!

Randy Johnson, the 6'10" lefty known as the "Big Unit" has won five Cy Young Awards. In the 1993 all-star game, the Phillies' best hitter, lefthander John Kruk, stepped up against Randy Johnson for the first time. Kruk was completely intimidated. He ducked and backed away from three straight pitches—but all three were strikes.

New York Mets

After both the Dodgers and Giants left New York for California in 1957, former fans wanted a replacement team. They didn't feel right rooting for the hated Yankees, the only New York team left! So, in 1962, the expansion Mets were formed. Their colors represent the teams they replaced: blue for the Dodgers and orange for the Giants.

In their first season, the Mets were awful. They won only 40 games—that's third worst in the modern era and still the worst since the 1930s. Even though they were bad, their fans loved them. After seven years of stinkage (they finished ninth or tenth out of ten in the league from 1962–1968), the Mets all of a sudden became good in the middle of the 1969 season. Behind the pitching of Tom Seaver and Jerry Koosman, the "Amazin'" Mets rallied past the Cubs to win their division, beat the Braves in the NLCS, and defeat the Orioles for their first World Championship. A few years later, in 1973, manager Yogi Berra took the team back to the World Series.

Nothing else good happened to the Mets until 1986, when their team of crazy guys defeated the Red Sox in a famous World Series. In 1999 and 2000 the Mets made the playoffs, but couldn't win a championship. Recently, the Mets have earned an unfortunate reputation, losing big leads in the standings in both 2007 and 2008. They moved to a new stadium in 2009 and spent a lot of money to bring in good pitchers in an unsuccessful attempt to return to the playoffs.

WORDS to KNOW

Expansion Team: Since 1962, the National League has added seven entirely new teams—not teams that moved from city to city or from league to league, but teams that were created from scratch. These teams are called "expansion" teams. They get their players by drafting from the existing teams. Expansion teams usually aren't very good for their first few years, but the Arizona Diamondbacks are a well-known exception.

New York Mets

Founded in 1962
2 World Championships (1969, 1986)
4 NL pennants

Famous Mets: Tom Seaver, 1967–1986

When "Tom Terrific" came up with the New York Mets in 1967, the Mets were the worst team in the major leagues. By 1969, they shocked everyone and won 100 games, with Tom Seaver winning 25 of them on the way to a World Championship. Seaver won his first of three Cy Young Awards that year and became the heart and soul of the Mets. In 1973 he led the Mets back to the World Series, but this time they lost to the A's. Much to the disappointment of Mets fans, he was traded away in 1977, returning only for a brief stint before his retirement in 1986. In his career, he won 20 or more games four times and led the league in strikeouts five times. Seaver retired as one of the 20 winningest pitchers of all time, and he sits sixth all-time in strikeouts. He was elected to the Hall of Fame in 1992 and even after that returned to the Mets one more time—only this time as an announcer.

Tom Seaver

W–L	ERA	K
311–205	2.86	3,640

Atlanta Braves

The Braves started out in Boston a long time ago. They were really, really good back in the 1800s, winning eight NL pennants between 1876 and 1899. They won the World Series in 1914 but weren't a contender again until the late 1940s.

The team moved to Milwaukee in 1953, and then became the first major league team in the South in 1966. The Braves were the joke of the National League through much of the 1970s and 1980s. But in 1990 the team hired general manager John Schuerholz away from Kansas City. Schuerholz named Bobby Cox his manager; Cox named Leo Mazzone his

 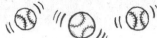
pitching coach. Under this leadership, the National League of the 1990s became the Atlanta Braves' League. Their phenomenal starting pitching won them their division every year between 1991 and 2005. They won the World Series title in 1995 when they beat the Cleveland Indians.

Atlanta Braves

Founded in 1876
Other names: Boston Red Caps, Boston Beaneaters, Boston Doves, Boston Rustlers, Boston Bees, Boston Braves, Milwaukee Braves
3 World Championships (1914, 1957, 1995)
17 NL pennants

Famous Braves: Hank Aaron, 1954–1976

Many people thought Babe Ruth's record of 714 career home runs would never be broken. Hank Aaron, nicknamed "the Hammer," knew better. Aaron played briefly in the Negro Leagues before being signed in 1954 by the Milwaukee Braves, who moved to Atlanta in 1966.

Aaron never topped 50 homers in a season, but he belted at least 25 home runs 18 times, with a high of 47. He also posted more than 120 RBIs seven times while setting the all-time career RBI record. By the time he finished his 23-year career back in Milwaukee as a member of the Brewers, he was also near the top in games played, hits, runs scored, and doubles. Aaron made the Hall of Fame in 1982.

Hank Aaron

HR	RBI	AVG
755	2,297	.305

Mazzone on Pitching

Most starting pitchers are afraid to throw too much between starts for fear of hurting their arms. Braves pitching coach Leo Mazzone thought that was ridiculous. He had his pitchers throw off the mound twice between starts, though only at about half speed. He seemed to know what he was doing; the Braves had the best starting pitching in the majors for more than a decade.

Play Ball

A baseball player must be sure to follow the rules of the game, or he could get sent to the dugout! You must carefully follow the directions below to learn the word that finishes the following popular saying: "Some people say that playing baseball is as American as eating _____."

1. Print the word BASEBALL.   B A S E B A L L

2. Switch the position of the first two letters.

3. Move the 5th letter between the 2nd and 3rd letters.

4. Switch the positions of the 4th and 8th letters.

5. Change the 6th letter to P.

6. Change the last letter to E.

7. Change both B s to P s.

8. Change the 7th letter to I.

Famous Braves: Greg Maddux, 1986–2008

He didn't have the blazing fastball of Randy Johnson, and he didn't put up amazing strikeout totals, but his secret to pitching was, as he put it, "making your strikes look like balls and your balls look like strikes." Greg Maddux was a very smart pitcher with tremendous control who knew how to get batters out. In 1997, for example, he walked only 14 batters in over 230 innings. He knew how to throw several pitches very well, and he could hit the corners of the plate with all of them. In 1995 and 1996, with the Braves, Greg went a combined 35–8 with a 1.60 ERA, capturing two of his four Cy Young Awards; in fact, some people in the late 1990s joked about renaming the award the "Greg Maddux Award."

Greg Maddux

W–L	ERA	K
355-227	3.16	3,371

FUN FACT

Brothers Who Hit Home Runs

There have been many brothers who played major league baseball, from Joe and Dom DiMaggio to Cal and Billy Ripken to Aaron and Bret Boone. But who were the brothers who hit the most combined home runs? Hank and Tommie Aaron. Hammerin' Hank hit 755, while Tommie added on 13 for a grand total of 768.

San Diego Padres

The expansion Padres went their first 15 years without a winning record. Then, all of a sudden, the team won their division, and beat the Cubs 3–2 in the NLCS in 1984. Unfortunately, they couldn't handle the Detroit Tigers in the World Series. But behind the hitting of Tony Gwynn and Steve Garvey, the team had brought successful baseball to San Diego for the first time. The Padres' 1998 season was eerily similar to 1984: Tony Gwynn's hitting led them to the playoffs, but in the World Series they had to face the Yankees at the height of their late-1990s dynasty. The Yanks won, four games to none.

More recently, the Padres won back-to-back division titles in 2005 and 2006—but they couldn't make it out of the first round of the playoffs either time. In 2007, the Padres' season came down to a one-game playoff with the Rockies for the division. Rocky Matt Holliday scored on a sacrifice fly in the ninth inning, though many fans still debate whether he touched home plate on his slide. That playoff loss took the wind out of the Padres' sails. In 2008, they lost almost 100 games to finish last in the NL west. They did better in 2009, finishing second in the NL west.

San Diego Padres

Founded in 1969
0 World Championships
2 NL pennants

Famous Padre: Tony Gwynn, 1982–2001

From the moment he came up to the big leagues, Gwynn was the best hitter in baseball and one of the best of all time. His career .338 average is up there with the greats of the early 1900s, and in 1994 he came within six points of batting .400, something that hadn't been done since 1941. Gwynn led the league in batting seven times, hitting over .360 four times. He could hit any pitch for a single or double and hardly ever struck out, which helps explain why he had over 3,000 career hits. In his younger years he was also a great base stealer and tremendous defensive player. Gwynn retired at the end of the 2001 season after 20 years with the San Diego Padres and 19 consecutive .300 seasons. He was inducted into the Hall of Fame in 2007; his son, Tony Gwynn Jr., now plays for the Padres.

Tony Gwynn

HR	RBI	AVG
135	1,138	.338

Cincinnati Reds

The original Cincinnati Red Stockings team was formed in 1863. In 1868, they became the first professional team ever—that means the Reds were the first team made up completely of players who were paid by the team owner. That original team stopped playing in 1870. A new Cincinnati Red Stockings team joined the National League in 1876, but that team was kicked out of the league. So today's Reds are really the third Cincinnati team to play professional baseball.

The Reds won their first World Championship in 1919, though it came under a cloud of suspicion: that was the year of the "Black Sox" scandal, when gamblers paid members of the Chicago White Sox to let the Reds win the Series. The most famous Reds teams in history played in the 1970s, when the team was known as the "Big Red Machine." Johnny Bench, Pete Rose, George Foster, and Tony Perez, among others, played for manager Sparky Anderson in an offensive lineup that struck fear into opposing pitchers. From 1961–1981, the Reds had nineteen winning seasons and seven playoff appearances.

Then the Reds had a few rough years, but they did much better when they brought back hometown hero Pete Rose to manage the team in 1985. In 1990, fiery Lou Pinella got his chance to manage the Reds, and he took them to the World Championship.

Since then, though, the Reds have had a long string of losing seasons. In fact, the team has not managed a winning

Player-manager: Occasionally the manager of a team is also a player, referred to as the player-manager. Hiring a player to manage the team used to be more common than it is now. The only player-manager in the last few decades was Pete Rose, who played for and managed the Reds in 1985 and 1986.

season since 2000, the second-longest current streak in the major leagues.

Cincinnati Reds

Founded in 1882
Other Names: Cincinnati Red Stockings, Cincinnati Redlegs
5 World Championships (1919, 1940, 1975, 1976, 1990)
10 NL pennants

Famous Red: Johnny Bench, 1967–1983

There was never a greater major league catcher than Johnny Bench. He broke into the major leagues in style when he was just 20 years old, making the all-star game and winning Rookie of the Year honors. In 1970, his third season, Bench won the National League MVP with 45 homers and 148 RBIs while leading the Reds to the World Series. Bench topped the 100 RBI mark on five occasions and was the main cog in Cincinnati's "Big Red Machine."

Besides his tremendous power hitting and many clutch hits, Bench was also an incredible defensive catcher and was known for his great throwing arm. He won 10 Gold Glove Awards as the best defensive catcher in the National League until injuries forced him to spend more time at third and first base. Two World Championships and consistently good play made Johnny Bench one of baseball's most popular players of the 1970s. But the injuries from catching caught up with him, and by age 35 Bench had to call it quits. He was elected to the Hall of Fame in 1985.

Johnny Bench

HR	RBI	AVG
389	1,376	.267

Los Angeles Dodgers

While the Dodgers were in their original home of Brooklyn, New York, they made it to the World Series eight times—but they only won once, in 1955. Just three seasons later, Brooklyn fans were heartbroken to see their team move thousands of miles away to Los Angeles.

But Southern California embraced their new team. The Dodgers won the Series in 1959, moved into a beautiful new stadium in 1962, and went back to the World Series in three of the next four years.

The Dodgers have historically been one of the best-run franchises in baseball. They are known for scouting good young pitchers from all over the world to play for their many minor league teams. In the 1960s, the famous Dodger pitchers were Sandy Koufax and Don Drysdale; in the 1980s, Fernando Valenzuela and Orel Hershiser. Hershiser was the ace of the pitching staff who, with the help of some power hitting from Kirk Gibson, won the Dodgers' most recent Championship, in 1988. Since then they've still been successful, making the playoffs six times.

The Beloved Bums from Brooklyn

Many people used to get around New York City by taking the trolley, which was a sort of train that ran at street level. People had to dodge the trolleys as they crossed streets—hence, the baseball team became the Brooklyn Trolley Dodgers. But fans sometimes referred to their team simply as the "Bums."

Los Angeles Dodgers

Founded in 1884
Other Names (all from their Brooklyn Days): Brooklyn Atlantics, Grays, Grooms, Bridegrooms, Superbas, Robins, and Dodgers
6 World Championships (1955, 1959, 1963, 1965, 1981, 1988)
22 NL pennants

Famous Dodger: Jackie Robinson, 1947–1956

Jackie Robinson broke into the major leagues with the Brooklyn Dodgers in 1947 at the age of 28 after several years in the Negro Leagues and two years in the minors. He led the league in stolen bases and won Rookie of the Year honors. But his entry into the majors was far more significant than his stats. Robinson broke the color barrier, becoming the first black player to play in the major leagues, at least since the late 1800s. Making a major statement for his race wasn't new to Robinson, who had been court-martialed out of the United States Army after he had refused to sit in the back of a bus because of the color of his skin.

The early days of his career were very difficult. Fans, players on other teams, and even many of his own teammates were cruel. Some players even started a petition that said they would not play in the game with him. But there were a lot of people on his side. He got support from some of his teammates, the Dodger manager and front office, and even the baseball commissioner. He also had the support and hopes of African Americans, who rooted passionately for him—even if he was playing against their own team! He also showed a great deal of sheer determination and proved himself as a first-rate ballplayer.

In 1949 Robinson hit .342, which led the league in batting, and he was named the MVP. In the next 10 years he would make a huge breakthrough for the game of baseball. Robinson's legacy continued long after his seven World Series appearances or his induction into the

Hall of Fame in 1962. In 1997, stadiums all over the country honored the 50-year anniversary of Robinson's achievement. His uniform number, 42, was retired throughout major league baseball. Though Jackie Robinson will be remembered foremost for breaking baseball's color barrier, it must be noted that his performance earned him recognition as one of the all-time greatest players of any color.

Jackie Robinson

HR	RBI	AVG
137	734	.311

Switch Hitter

Can you see the 10 differences between the two pictures of this batter?

HINT: It doesn't count that he's facing in different directions—that's what a switch hitter does!

Who's Who?

Some baseball nicknames are easy to guess. For example, almost all players who have had the last name "Rhodes" have gotten the nickname "Dusty." See how many of the famous nicknames on the left you can match with the real names on the right. Put the number of the correct nickname on the line in front of each real name.

HINT: For those names you can't figure out, or don't know already, look through this book. They're in here somewhere!

1. The Big Train
2. Tom Terrific
3. Cyclone
4. Joltin' Joe
5. Double X
6. Mr. October
7. The Mick
8. Say Hey Kid
9. Stan The Man
10. Charlie Hustle
11. Wizard of Oz
12. The Big Unit
13. The Rocket

___ Cy Young
___ Jimmy Foxx
___ Joe DiMaggio
___ Mickey Mantle
___ Ozzie Smith
___ Pete Rose
___ Randy Johnson
___ Reggie Jackson
___ Roger Clemens
___ Stan Musial
___ Tom Seaver
___ Walter Johnson
___ Willie Mays

Look! It's "Bubbles" MacCoy!

58

Milwaukee Brewers

In 1969, the American League added two teams, one in Kansas City and one in Seattle. But the Seattle team went bankrupt in just one year. They survived by moving to Milwaukee for the 1970 season—which is where they've stayed ever since. Problem is, the Brewers have rarely been a good team. They went to the playoffs for the first time in 1981, and they made it again in 1982—but their next playoff appearance wasn't until 2008. The Brewers are the only team ever to switch leagues. In 1997, when the Devil Rays and Diamondbacks were formed, the Brewers switched to the National League so that each league would have an even number of teams.

Hall of Fame Designated Hitter

Brewer Paul Molitor hit for a lifetime average of .306. He played most of his career in Milwaukee, leading the team to its only World Series appearance in 1982. He was elected to the Hall of Fame in 2004. Since the Brewers had usually used him as a designated hitter, that's the position on his plaque—the only player in the Hall as a DH.

Famous Brewers: The Sausages

At old County Stadium, the scoreboard used to show a cartoon race between different kinds of sausages. The fans would pick which sausage they wanted to win and cheer for him like they would at a horse race. In 1994, the scoreboard race was replaced by an actual race between people wearing sausage costumes. Since then, after the sixth inning of every Brewers home game, the sausages race around the field and the fans root for their favorite.

Originally, three sausages took part in the race: the Bratwurst, the Polish Sausage, and the Italian Sausage. Nowadays, two more sausages run as well: the Hot Dog, and the Chorizo. In 2009, the Hot Dog won the most races and captured the Sausage Race title.

Pittsburgh Pirates

The Pirates reached their peak in the 1970s, when they rivaled the Big Red Machine as the team of the decade. They went to the playoffs six times in ten years, winning the World Series twice. Their team combined sluggers like Willie Stargell with the speedster Omar Moreno. In 1979, they chose the disco song "We Are Family" as their theme song, playing it at every game—and fans still sing it today.

The Pirates had one more resurgence, in the early 1990s under manager Jim Leyland. A young Barry Bonds led the team to the NLCS three straight years. But the Pirates' hopes came crashing down in Game 7 in 1992, when the Braves scored three runs in the bottom of the ninth to win the game and the series, the last on a single by Francisco Cabrera. Barry Bonds had a chance to throw out slow-running Sid Bream at home to keep the game alive, but his throw was just barely late.

Bream's run seemed to mark the end of the team's success. Bonds left for San Francisco the very next year. Leyland left a few years later. And the Pirates haven't had a winning season since. In 2009, the Pirates had their seventeenth consecutive losing season—the longest losing streak in the history of North American professional sports.

Pittsburgh Pirates

Founded in 1892
Other Names: Pittsburgh Alleghenys
5 World Championships (1909, 1925, 1960, 1971, 1979)
9 NL pennants

Famous Pirate: Roberto Clemente, 1955–1972

Roberto Clemente was a tremendous all-around ballplayer. Not only could he hit for a high average, but he had power and was a super defensive outfielder, winning 12 Gold Gloves. He joined the Pirates in the mid-1950s as a 20-year-old rookie from Puerto Rico. He went on to become the greatest player from Puerto Rico and the first Hispanic player elected to the Hall of Fame. Clemente led the National League in batting four times in the 1960s, and four times he had more than 200 hits in a season. He appeared in two World Series for the Pirates and batted .362 overall, helping lead the Pirates to the title in 1971.

Clemente became one of the few players to get his 3,000th hit, which came at the end of the 1972 season. It would be his last hit ever. On New Year's Eve of that year he was on his way to deliver supplies to victims of a severe earthquake in Nicaragua when the plane he was on crashed. Clemente died at age 38 but is remembered as a hero both on and off the field.

Roberto Clemente

HR	RBI	AVG
240	1,305	.317

Washington Nationals

One of the 1969 expansion franchises went to Montreal, the first team ever in Canada. The Montreal Expos played for many years—mainly unsuccessfully—in the depressing Olympic Stadium. Behind

Famous Fungo!

Can you match the silly answers to the funny riddles?

1. What do you call a baseball player who only hits flap-jacks?

2. What do you call a baseball player who throws dairy products?

3. What do you call a dog that stands behind home plate?

____ **A milk pitcher!**

____ **A catcher's mutt!**

____ **A pancake batter!**

A "fungo" is actually a ball hit to the infield during fielding practice. Fungoes are hit with a special thin, light bat called a "fungo stick"!

FUN FACT

1994 Expo All-Stars

That 1994 Expos team, the one that went on strike and missed their chance at the World Series, included seven players who went on to be all-stars—with other teams.

Moises Alou and Pedro Martinez, the Expos looked like the best team in baseball in 1994. But the players went on strike that year, the World Series was canceled, and the Expos couldn't afford to keep their good players. Ten mostly losing seasons later, the team packed up and moved to Washington, D.C., where they renamed themselves the Nationals. The team hasn't done any better in Washington—they've had no winning seasons and were the worst team in baseball in 2008 and 2009.

Washington Nationals

Founded in 1969
Other Names: Montreal Expos
0 World Championships
0 NL pennants

Chicago Cubs

The Cubs were the best team in baseball a century ago, winning the World Series in both 1908 and 1909. They got back to the Series seven more times—but then the Curse of the Billy Goat struck. The story is that Billy Sianis, the owner of the famous Billy Goat Tavern in Chicago, brought an actual billy goat to a World Series game in 1945. Other fans didn't like the way the goat smelled, and Sianis was kicked out. According to legend, Sianis was so angry he cursed the team, saying, "Them Cubs, they ain't gonna win no more!"

He was right. The Cubs didn't even make the playoffs for the next 38 years—not even in 1969, when they collapsed after building a huge lead in the division. They were winning the deciding game of the 1984 NLCS, but they blew a 3–0 lead after a ground ball went through an infielder's legs.

Similarly, in 2003, the Cubs were up 3–0 in the game that could send them to the Series—but a spectator wouldn't let a Cub catch a foul ball, the shortstop let a ball through his legs, and the Cubs lost. The Cubs have fielded very good teams recently, but they lost in the first playoff round in both 2007 and 2008. The team has gone 101 years without a championship, the longest in all of professional sports. Many fans believe that they will continue to lose until the Curse of the Billy Goat is reversed.

Chicago Cubs

Founded in 1876
Other Names: Chicago White Stockings, Chicago Colts, Chicago Orphans
2 World Championships (1907, 1908)
16 NL pennants

Mr. Cub: Ernie Banks, 1953–1971

Ernie Banks began his career in the Negro Leagues in 1950. He joined the Cubs as their shortstop in 1953. Banks was best known for his deep love of the game of baseball, particularly where the Chicago Cubs were involved. "Let's play two," he used to say on beautiful afternoons. It was Banks who first called Wrigley Field the "Friendly Confines," a nickname for the ballpark that's used regularly even today. In 1982, the Cubs retired Banks's number 14—the first number they had ever retired. A bronze statue of Ernie Banks stands outside Wrigley Field in honor of the man called "Mr. Cub."

FUN FACT

Wrigley Field

The Cubs started playing at Wrigley in 1916. Since then, Wrigley Field has become more than just a ballpark; it's a landmark in Chicago. The ivy-covered brick outfield walls, an old hand-operated scoreboard, and rooftop views from the surrounding apartment buildings all add to the unique atmosphere of the most popular park in the National League. Until 1988, all games at Wrigley were day games; even now, the Cubs play more day games than any other team.

Chapter 4
The American League

The American League

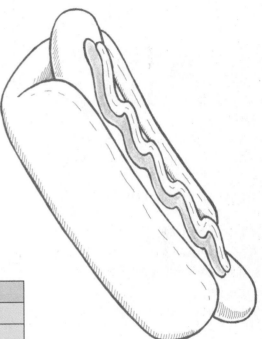

The American League is sometimes called the "junior circuit," while the National League is the "senior circuit." Why? Because the AL was formed 25 years after the NL. Of course, the AL has still been around for as long as anyone can remember. It began in 1901 when the old "Western League" chose a new name, and decided that they were just as much a major league as the NL.

There were eight teams in the original American League. All eight teams are still around, though only the Tigers are still in the same city with the same name.

The Original 1876 American League

1876 Team Name	Modern Team Name
Chicago White Stockings	Chicago White Sox
Boston Americans	Boston Red Sox
Detroit Tigers	Detroit Tigers
Philadelphia Athletics	Oakland Athletics
Baltimore Orioles	New York Yankees
Washington Senators	Minnesota Twins
Cleveland Blues	Cleveland Indians
Milwaukee Brewers	Baltimore Orioles

Fourteen teams make up the American League today. The only major difference between an AL team and an NL team is the use of the designated hitter. Pitchers don't bat in games played in AL ballparks. Nowadays, most people think the American League has better teams than the National League. For example, the AL has won twelve straight all-star games; in interleague play, the AL has beaten the NL in seven of the last nine years. Still, recent World Series champions have come from both leagues.

FUN FACT

What's a Devil Ray, anyway?

The Devil Rays were named after a strange sort of fish that looks more like a flying squirrel than a fish. In 2007, the team decided that they shouldn't be named after fish. Now the "Rays" refer to rays of light.

Tampa Bay Rays

In 1998, the last time that major league baseball expanded, the Tampa Bay Devil Rays were born. While fans were excited to have major league baseball in town, their team took a while to rack up wins. They finished in last place in the AL East each of their first six years. In 2003, the team brought in the famous manager Lou Pinella, who had won the World Series with the Reds and taken the Mariners to the playoffs. But the team still couldn't improve. In fact, 2004 was the only year they ever finished out of last place— and they finished next-to-last.

Pinella left in 2006, new owners and a new general manager took over . . . and the team still finished last. But talented young players like Carl Crawford and Scott Kazmir seemed likely to bring future success. Sure enough, everything came together in 2008. They won their division and made it to the World Series. They lost 4–1 to the Phillies, though three of the four losses were close. Now the Rays have the prospects of many good years ahead of them.

Tampa Bay Rays

Founded in 1998
Other Names: Tampa Bay Devil Rays
0 World Championships
1 AL pennant

Boston Red Sox

The Red Sox moved into Fenway Park in 1912 and won the World Series four of the next seven years. Pitcher and all-time home run king Babe Ruth was the team's best player and a fan favorite. But in 1919, owner Harry Frazee traded

Babe Ruth to the Yankees. Whether as a direct result of that mistake or not, the Red Sox didn't win another World Series for 86 years.

The Sox came close a few times, only to lose in heart-breaking fashion. In 1975 they pushed the Reds to Game 7. In 1978, they lost a one-game playoff to the Yankees on a home run by Bucky Dent. In 1986, a ground ball through Bill Buckner's legs in the sixth game of the World Series allowed the Mets to score the winning run. In 2003, Yankee Bret Boone eliminated the Sox with a walk-off home run in Game 7 of the ALCS. The Red Sox were cursed.

The curse seemed to continue in 2004. The Yankees won the first three games of the ALCS—including a blistering 19–8 victory in Game 3. No team in the history of major league baseball had ever come back from a 3–0 deficit to win a seven-game series, but the Red Sox beat the odds and took the series. They went on to dispatch the Cardinals in four games to claim the World Championship. The Red Sox have continued to be a dominant power in the AL. They won another World Championship in 2007 and returned to the playoffs in 2008 and 2009.

WORDS to KNOW

Green Monster: Famous Fenway Park is one of the majors' two ancient ballparks. To make the field fit inside the available space, the left field fence is very, very shallow—about 305 feet. So, to prevent a gazillion home runs to left field, the fence there is 37 feet high. Because the wall is so huge, and because it's painted green, it's called the "Green Monster."

Boston Red Sox

Founded in 1901
Other Names: Boston Americans
7 World Championships (1903, 1912, 1915, 1916, 1918, 2004, 2007)
12 AL pennants

Famous Red Sox: Ted Williams, 1939–1960

Ted Williams, known as "the Splendid Splinter," was one of the most remarkable hitters ever. He hit for power, for a

high average, and rarely ever struck out. In fact, after his career he wrote a book called *The Science of Hitting*, which is still a terrific book to read for anyone who wants to learn to be a better hitter. As a rookie in 1939, Williams hit .327 and batted .406 in 1941. No one has batted over .400 for an entire season since Williams did it—more than sixty years ago! In 1942, Williams not only led the league in batting average again, but also led with 37 home runs and 137 runs batted in, winning the Triple Crown. Williams's career was interrupted twice, once when he was drafted into the Navy for World War II, and again when he volunteered to serve in the Korean War. Both times he returned to baseball to have great seasons. Williams finally called it quits at age 42 and was inducted into the Hall of Fame in 1965.

Ted Williams

HR	RBI	AVG
521	1,839	.344

Detroit Tigers

The Tigers franchise started off strong in the early 1900s, winning three AL pennants behind the meanest ballplayer ever, Ty Cobb. The team has had successful seasons every decade or two throughout its history. It seems like famous managers have been the key to their most recent successes. In 1971, the Tigers hired Billy Martin, who took them to the playoffs in 1972, but then left. In 1979, Sparky Anderson took over the team; in 1984, he led the Tigers to the World Championship, becoming the first manager to win the World Series in both the AL and the NL. But then, the Tigers' fortunes soured. In 2003, they were the laughing stock of baseball when they lost 119 games—the second-worst record

in history, behind only the 1962 expansion Mets. But former Pirates manager Jim Leyland came aboard in 2006 and turned the team around. They made it to the World Series, but fell to the Cardinals in five games.

Detroit Tigers

Founded in 1901
4 World Championships (1935, 1945, 1968, 1984)
10 AL pennants

Famous Tigers: Ty Cobb, 1905–1928

Cobb was one of the toughest players of all time. He worked very hard and spent hours practicing hitting, sliding, and throwing to make it to the major leagues in 1905 at the age of 18. The hard work paid off. Cobb played 24 years, almost all for the Tigers, and hit under .300 just once, as a rookie. He batted over .400 three times and led the league in batting average 12 times on his way to an incredible .367 career batting average. Cobb was also one of the best base stealers ever, stealing nearly 900 bases.

Cobb's great hitting made him one of the first five players elected to the Hall of Fame. The fans enjoyed watching Cobb play, but he rarely got along with his teammates, and opposing players hated him. He would sharpen his spikes before the game and then slide in hard, feet first. Cobb said when he was older that if he had one thing he could do differently it would be to have more friends.

Ty Cobb

HR	RBI	AVG
118	1,961	.367

FUN FACT

Thirty-Game Winner

The last pitcher to top the thirty-win mark was Denny McLain, who won thirty-one games for the Detroit Tigers in 1968. He's the only pitcher to win more than thirty games in a season in more than forty years!

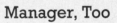

Manager, Too

Cobb not only played for the Tigers, but for six years was a player-manager for them, too, amassing a 479–444 record. He took the Tigers as high as second place in the American League.

Chicago White Sox

The White Sox are sometimes referred to as the "South Siders." The Chicago Cubs play at Wrigley Field, on the north side of the city; the White Sox play at a new version of Comiskey Park on the south side, and most of their fans come from the south side. The team won the World Series twice in their early days, but then got involved in the worst scandal in the history of baseball. In 1919, eight White Sox players took money from gamblers and agreed to lose the Series to the Reds. These players were banned from baseball for life—and the White Sox didn't manage to win a World Series again until 2005.

Before their championship, the Sox might have been best known for their weird owner, Bill Veeck. He made the team wear shorts as their uniform for a season. He held "Disco Demolition Night," where fans were supposed to bring music that would be burned in a big pile between games of a doubleheader. (That didn't work out too well.) Eventually Veeck sold the team, and they actually won a few division titles in the 1980s and 1990s.

Chicago White Sox

Founded in 1901
3 World Championships (1906, 1917, 2005)
6 AL pennants

New York Yankees

The Yankees are the most successful major league team. They are the best-known team nationally—and even worldwide. Any time the Yankees are the visiting team, that game is almost guaranteed to sell out. The Yanks have

been so good through their history that it's probably easier to list the few times when they *haven't* been in the playoffs: 1965–1974 and 1982–1994 represent their longest times out of the playoffs since 1921. In 1996, the Yankees won the World Series under manager Joe Torre, and they won four of the next five Series as well. Crazily enough, some folks think the Yankees have been disappointing since then, because even though they've been in the playoffs every year except 2008, they have only won one World Championship since 2000.

Yes, the Yankees expect to win the World Series every year. They can do that because they have more money than any other team in baseball. They play in the country's biggest city; the Yankees even have their own television station. So,

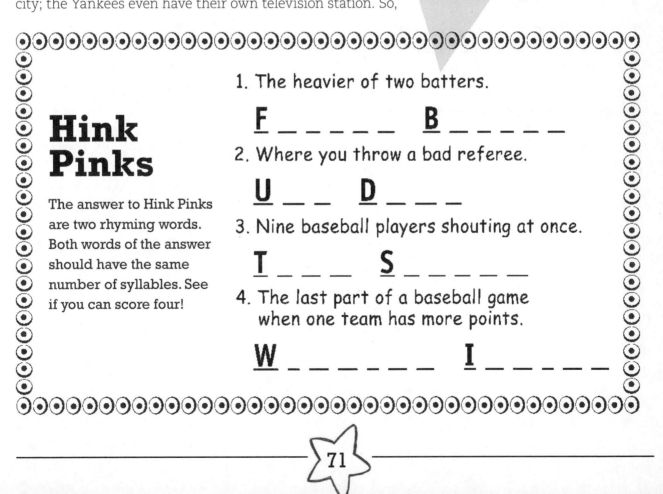

Hink Pinks

The answer to Hink Pinks are two rhyming words. Both words of the answer should have the same number of syllables. See if you can score four!

1. The heavier of two batters.

F _ _ _ _ _   B _ _ _ _ _

2. Where you throw a bad referee.

U _ _   D _ _ _ _

3. Nine baseball players shouting at once.

T _ _ _   S _ _ _ _ _

4. The last part of a baseball game when one team has more points.

W _ _ _ _ _ _   I _ _ _ _ _ _

Baseball Diamond

Can you find six common baseball terms hidden in the diamond grid? Start at a letter and move one space at a time in any direction to a touching letter. You may not use the same letter twice in a word, but you can cross over your own path.

HINT:
One of the terms is an abbreviation!

when the Yankees see a player they'd like to have, they usually give him as much money as he wants.

A huge number of the game's greatest players wore Yankee uniforms, too many to write about here. Babe Ruth and Lou Gehrig led the famous teams of the late 1920s. Joltin' Joe DiMaggio played center field in the 1940s; Mickey Mantle took over in the 1950s. Roger Maris hit 61 home runs in 1961, breaking Ruth's record. In the 1970s, Yankee Reggie Jackson became known as "Mr. October" for his postseason heroics. The great first baseman Don Mattingly joined the team in 1982 and retired in 1995—after playing in only one playoff series. Now, team captain Derek Jeter is the best known and most loved Yankee, the most recent in a long line of the game's best.

New York Yankees

Founded in 1901
Other Names: Baltimore Orioles, New York Highlanders
27 World Championships (1923, 1927, 1928, 1932, 1936, 1937, 1938, 1939, 1941, 1943, 1947, 1949, 1950, 1951, 1952, 1953, 1956, 1958, 1961, 1962, 1977, 1978, 1996, 1998, 1999, 2000, 2009)
40 AL pennants

Famous Yankees: Babe Ruth, 1914–1935

It's almost impossible to find anyone who hasn't heard of "the Babe." Also nicknamed the Bambino, George Herman "Babe" Ruth could do it all. He began as a pitcher with the Boston Red Sox before moving to the outfield. He went on to change the face of baseball. When Ruth led the major leagues with 29 home runs in 1919, it was the first time a player had hit more than 25 in a season. He was traded to the Yankees, where he became the greatest home run hitter ever.

Ruth's 714 home runs stood as the record until Hank Aaron passed that mark in 1974. Had Ruth not been a pitcher for several years, who knows how many he would have hit. He led the league in home runs (or tied for the lead) twelve times. He also batted .342 for his career and is still considered by most baseball historians as the greatest baseball player ever. Ruth led the Yankees to one World Series title after another. An often-told story says that in one World Series against the Cubs, Ruth stepped up to the plate,

pointed to the bleachers where he was going to hit a home run . . . and then did just that.

Beyond baseball, Ruth was an enormously popular celebrity and was treated like royalty. The Babe enjoyed all the publicity and excitement that surrounded him. It was said that "as he moved, center stage moved with him." Ruth retired in 1935 and was one of the first five players elected to the Hall of Fame in 1939.

Babe Ruth

HR	RBI	AVG	W–L	ERA	K
714	2,213	.342	94–46	2.28	488

Famous Yankee: Lou Gehrig, 1923–1939

Gehrig was called the Iron Horse because he was always in the lineup. He batted right after "the Babe" in the great Yankees lineup and played in Ruth's shadow. Nonetheless, Gehrig was as awesome a hitter as anyone. For 14 consecutive years he drove in more than 100 runs, topping 170 three times and setting an American League record with 184 in 1931. He could do it all. He got more than 200 hits eight times, hit 40 home runs five times, and batted over .300 for 13 consecutive years. His 23 grand slam home runs is the all-time high.

Despite all of his amazing accomplishments, Gehrig is best known for two things. He began a streak in 1925 where he played every single game until 1939, or 2,130 consecutive games, a record most people thought would never be broken. (Cal Ripken Jr. has since topped that incredible record.) Unfortunately, the other thing Gehrig is best remembered for is the reason he removed himself from the lineup eight games into the 1939 season. Gehrig had been suffering from

Pride of the Yankees

The movie *Pride of the Yankees* is a marvelous, deeply touching story of Gehrig's life.

an unknown disease, which later became known as Lou Gehrig's disease. He retired from baseball in May 1939, and in July he famously described himself as the "luckiest man on earth" for the opportunity to have played for the Yankees, and to have been loved by the fans and by his wife. Less than two years later he died at the age of 37. He was elected into the Hall of Fame in 1939.

Lou Gehrig

HR	RBI	AVG
493	1,995	.340

Los Angeles Angels

The Angels play in Anaheim, which is about an hour away from Los Angeles, California. The team was known as the California Angels for many years. As an expansion team in 1961, the Angels won 70 games, still the best season ever for a first-year expansion team. But for a long time, the team was noted more for its interesting stadium with the enormous "A" in the outfield than for any on-field success. In 2000, former Dodger catcher Mike Scioscia came on board as manager. He and slugger Vladimir Guerrero led the team to five playoff appearances this decade, including their only World Championship in 2002.

Los Angeles Angels

Founded in 1961
Other Names: California Angels, Anaheim Angels
1 World Championship (2002)
1 AL pennant

Clever T-shirt

When the Angels made their second name change in just a few years, deciding to call themselves the Los Angeles Angels of Anaheim, the Dodgers decided to have a bit of fun at the Angels' expense. They printed T-shirts that said "Los Angeles Dodgers of Los Angeles."

Famous Angels: Nolan Ryan, 1966–1993

Nolan Ryan was truly a flame-thrower, firing the ball harder and faster than anyone had ever seen. When Ryan came up with the Mets in 1966 he could throw very hard, but he had control problems and walked a lot of hitters. In 1972 the Mets traded him to the California Angels, and there he turned into a big winner and became the king of strikeouts. He led the league 11 times in strikeouts; in 1973, he struck out a whopping 383 hitters. While most pitchers would be thrilled to throw one no-hitter in their careers, Ryan threw seven—a major league record.

A native of Texas, Ryan was excited when he got to play for the Houston Astros, where he topped Walter Johnson's long-held all-time career strikeout record in 1983 at the age of 36. Ryan, however, was far from done. Somehow, no matter how hard he threw, his arm never seemed to get tired. He surprised everyone by pitching in the big leagues for another ten years until he finally retired at age 46. By that time he had over 5,000 strikeouts, far more than anyone else. He made the Hall of Fame in 1999.

Nolan Ryan

W–L	ERA	K
324–292	3.19	5,386

Cleveland Indians

After their 1948 championship and a 1954 AL pennant, the Indians fell into a 40-year funk. They played at the old Cleveland Municipal Stadium, located off the shore of Lake Erie where the winds blew cold and the fans barely ever

WORDS to KNOW

No-Hitter: When a pitcher allows no hits in a game, it's called a no-hitter. It's still a no-hitter if the pitcher walks batters, or if batters reach base on fielding errors. In fact, it's possible for a pitcher to pitch a no-hitter but still lose the game!

showed up. The team was so bad that an entire movie, 1989's *Major League*, made fun of their awfulness.

In 1994, though, the city opened new Jacobs Field in downtown Cleveland. The very next year, the Indians made it to the World Series. With the support of a sold-out crowd every night, the Indians made the playoffs pretty much every year until 2002. The Indians won their division again in 2007, and led the Red Sox 3–1 with a chance to go to the World Series, but the Red Sox came back to win three blowouts.

Cleveland Indians

Founded in 1961
Other Names: Cleveland Blues, Bronchos, Naps
2 World Championships (1920, 1948)
5 AL pennants

Famous Indians: Satchel Paige, 1926–1953

Satchel Paige was a genuine baseball superstar. He had a long career, during which an estimated 10 million people watched him pitch—in person, since he played most of his games before they were shown on television! Paige played for a variety of Negro League teams from 1926 to 1947, moving from team to team depending on who could pay him the most money. Americans, black or white, were willing to pay to see Paige pitch. His reputation as one of the greatest pitchers in baseball was well established before World War II, during which he raised money for the war effort through his pitching exhibitions. He played with Negro League all-stars in competitive exhibition games against major leaguers. Finally, after Jackie Robinson broke in with the Dodgers, Paige was signed to a major-league

FUN FACT

Sellout Streak

From 1995 until 2001, every seat at Jacobs Field was sold out every night, for 455 games in a row. Therefore, the Indians retired the number 455 in honor of their fans.

contract with the Cleveland Indians in 1948 at age 42. He played two seasons with the Indians, then moved with owner Bill Veeck to the St. Louis Browns, where he made the all-star team. His career totals look poor compared to the other pitchers in this list; but bear in mind, Paige put up these numbers over only five seasons, and he was 47 years old during that last season. One can only imagine the kind of career stats Paige could have earned had he played all of those 27 years in the major leagues.

Satchel Paige

W–L	ERA	K
28–31	3.29	288

Major league totals only

Toronto Blue Jays

The Blue Jays joined the American League as an expansion franchise to become the second major league team outside the United States. Now that the Montreal Expos have moved to Washington, D.C., the Blue Jays are the *only* Canadian team. They didn't begin to make their mark until the late 1980s and early 1990s, when they became one of the best in the majors.

In 1989, the Blue Jays moved from the old, cold, and ugly Exhibition Stadium into a new stadium, called SkyDome. This special building had the first-ever retractable roof in a domed stadium. The Blue Jays could play indoors when it was too cold or wet to be comfortable outside, but on warm summer nights, they could open the roof! The Blue Jays made the playoffs in 1989, 1991, 1992, and 1993. They won a dramatic World Series in 1992, when almost all the games were decided by just one run. They followed that up with

Oh, Canada!

Baseball games traditionally begin with the singing of the U.S. national anthem, "The Star-Spangled Banner." But if the Blue Jays are in town, you'll also hear the Canadian anthem "Oh, Canada!"

a second World Championship in 1993, when Joe Carter's Game 6 homer ended both the game and the Series.

Toronto Blue Jays

Founded in 1977
2 World Championships (1992, 1993)
2 AL pennants

Minnesota Twins

The Washington Senators were one of the AL's original eight teams. In 1961, the Senators moved to the twin cities of Minneapolis–St. Paul, Minnesota, and became the Twins. The team originally played in cold Metropolitan Stadium, but moved indoors to the Metrodome in 1982.

The Metrodome helped the team win their first World Series in Minnesota. In 1987, the Twins had the best home record in the league (56–21) but on the road they were 33–52. In the playoffs and the World Series they won every game in the Metrodome. Similarly, in 1991, the Twins beat the Braves 4–3 in the World Series, winning all four games in the Metrodome. The Twins are moving into a new outdoor stadium in 2010, but the Metrodome will always hold a dear place in Twins fans' hearts.

Minnesota Twins

Founded in 1901
Other Names: Washington Senators, Washington Nationals
3 World Championships (1924, 1987, 1991)
6 AL pennants

Famous Twins: Kirby Puckett, 1984–1995

Though he was only 5'8", Kirby Puckett played baseball like a giant. His batting average was .288 in his *worst* season. He also hit for power, hitting double-digit home runs in nine of his 12 seasons. In addition to his batting skills, Puckett was known as an outstanding defensive outfielder. Highlights of his playing days show him crashing into the Metrodome's "Hefty Bag" outfield wall, making catch after spectacular catch. The highlight of Puckett's career came in the 1991 World Series. In Game 6, he drove in a run with a triple; he made an amazing catch in front of the left-center field wall; and he won the game with a walk-off home run in the eleventh inning.

In 1995, Puckett was hit in the head by a pitch, which broke his jaw. Puckett developed eye problems and never played a major league game again. He became one of the youngest hall of famers ever when he was elected on the first ballot in 2001. Kirby Puckett died of a stroke in 2006 at age 45.

Kirby Puckett

HR	RBI	AVG
207	1,085	.318

Oakland Athletics

The American League club in Philadelphia was called the Athletics. Newspaper writers, always looking for a way to shorten a team's name, started calling them the "A's." The team was very successful in its early years, but after several poor decades, they moved to Kansas City in 1955. Their luck didn't get any better there. Finally, in 1968, the team moved west to Oakland. There, they started running the team smartly and started winning championships again.

The A's dominated the early 1970s, winning the Series three straight years—including a victory over the Big Red Machine. The "bash brothers," Jose Canseco and Mark McGwire, took them to the playoffs four times in the 1980s and 1990s, resulting in one more Championship. In 1997, the A's hired Billy Beane as general manager. He figured out how to help the team win without spending a lot of money. His moves worked out well, as the A's made the playoffs four years straight starting in 2000.

Oakland Athletics

Founded in 1901
Other Names: Philadelphia Athletics, Kansas City Athletics
9 World Championships (1910, 1911, 1913, 1929, 1930, 1972, 1973, 1974, 1989)
15 AL pennants

Famous Athletics: Reggie Jackson, 1967–1987

Reggie Jackson earned the nickname "Mr. October" because he was awesome when it was World Series time (in October). A great power hitter even in his rookie year in 1967, Jackson went on to lead the league in home runs four times during his career and ended up sixth on the all-time list when he retired. Jackson helped the A's win three consecutive World Series championships in 1972, 1973, and 1974. He later joined the Yankees and helped lead them to the World Series three times and to win two more World Championships. Reggie struck out a lot and wasn't a great defensive star, but when it was an important game, he was at his best. In Game 6 of the 1977 World Series, Jackson had what many consider the single best World Series game of any hitter ever. He hit three tremendous home runs and

drove in five runs in the game. Jackson was outspoken and very popular everywhere he went through his entire career. He made the Hall of Fame in 1993.

Reggie Jackson

HR	RBI	AVG
563	1,702	.262

Kansas City Royals

The Royals were once a proud franchise. The team was named for the American Royal, a yearly Kansas City Rodeo, and the Royals wear white home uniforms trimmed with royal blue. Under managers Whitey Herzog and Dick Howser, they finished either first or second in their division every year between 1975 and 1985, when they won their only World Series. After that, though, uncertain ownership and poor decisions about their players put the Royals at the bottom of the league for many years. Since 1990, the Royals have had just three winning seasons and have not even come close to the playoffs. The team hopes that young players like center-fielder David DeJesus can return them to their past successes.

Kansas City Royals

Founded in 1969
1 World Championship (1985)
2 AL pennants

Famous Royals: George Brett, 1973–1993

George Brett spent his entire career as a Royal, and that career coincided with the best years of the Kansas City Royals franchise. He was a better than .300 hitter who also hit 15–20

Waterfall in the Outfield

In 1973, the Royals moved into Royals Stadium, still one of the most beautiful major league parks. It was eventually renamed for longtime owner Ewing Kauffman. There aren't very many seats in the outfield at Royals Stadium. Instead, the Water Spectacular puts on a huge waterfall show in between innings. A home run by the Royals can end up splashing!

home runs every year. As if that weren't good enough, he was even better in the postseason. In the 1977 ALCS, he hit three home runs in the same game; he and teammate Hal McRae both rank top-ten all time in World Series batting average.

Despite his awesome career, Brett might be best remembered for the pine tar incident. In 1983, he hit a go-ahead home run against the Yankees, but he was called out for using an illegal bat that had too much sticky pine tar on it. Brett charged the umpire in a crazy, spitting rage. As it turned out, the commissioner later decided that the rule about pine tar on bats wasn't clear, so the home run counted. George Brett is the only Royal in the Hall of Fame. He was inducted in 1999.

George Brett

HR	RBI	AVG
317	1,595	.305

Baltimore Orioles

Though it's rare to hear about it nowadays, for 52 years the Orioles played in St. Louis as the Browns. In 1954 the team realized it couldn't compete with the Cardinals for St. Louis fans, so it left for Baltimore, changing its name and even trading most of its best-known players. The move didn't help the team win. For its first decade in Baltimore, the Orioles were just as bad as the Browns had been. But that all changed in 1965 when the Orioles traded for young slugger Frank Robinson, who led the league in home runs, RBIs, and batting average in 1966—the same year he led his team to its first World Championship. The Orioles continued to dominate under the feisty Earl Weaver, who was an excellent manager even if he was known for being a complete jerk to

umpires. Lately, though, the Orioles have been better known for their poor choices of players than for winning baseball.

Baltimore Orioles

Founded in 1901
Other Names: Milwaukee Brewers, St. Louis Browns
3 World Championships (1966, 1970, 1983)
7 AL pennants

Famous Orioles: Cal Ripken Jr., 1981–2001

Cal Ripken Jr. was named Rookie of the Year in 1982 and MVP in 1983 and 1991. He established himself as one of the top players in modern baseball. Ripken always came to play—and play hard—day in and day out. In late 1995, he went from a star to a legend when he broke a record that most thought could never be topped. Ripken played in his 2,131st consecutive game, breaking the iron horse record set by the late great Lou Gehrig. Ripken played another 501 more consecutive games before taking himself out of the lineup in September 1998.

During the 2001 season, Ripken announced his retirement after twenty years with the Orioles. He was inducted into the Hall of Fame in 2007. In his career, Ripken played in 3,001 games and had 3,184 hits, 431 home runs, and nearly 1,700 RBIs. He was also one of the best-liked and most respected individuals who ever played in the major leagues.

Cal Ripken Jr.

HR	RBI	AVG
431	1,695	.276

Seattle Mariners

The Mariners were born as an expansion franchise in 1977. They struggled to win for years and years, until a new owner brought in manager Lou Piniella in 1993. Piniella, along with some seriously talented players, took Seattle to the playoffs four times in the late 1990s. But the Mariners could never get to the World Series. One by one, the star players left. Ken Griffey Jr. went to the Reds; Alex Rodriguez went to the Rangers; Tino Martinez went to the Yankees; Randy Johnson went to the Astros. The .330 hitting outfielder Ichiro Suzuki remains on the team, and today the team is rebuilding around him.

Seattle Mariners

Seattle Mariners
Founded in 1977
0 World Championships
0 AL pennants

FUN FACT

The Mariner Moose

In 1990 the Mariners chose the Moose as their official mascot. He appears at all home games, as well as on television ads and at community events. The Mariner Moose has earned fame for his recklessness. He broke his ankle when he crashed into the outfield wall on roller skates, and he nearly ran down one of the Red Sox on his cart.

Texas Rangers

In 1961, the old Washington Senators, which had been around since 1901, moved to Minnesota to become the Twins. But a new Senators team was awarded to Washington as part of the AL's expansion that year. That team was terrible. The owners didn't know much about running a baseball team, and they didn't have any money to spend on players, anyway. In 1972, the team moved to Arlington, Texas, which is near Dallas. Though the newly named Texas Rangers weren't always in last place as the Senators had been, the team still never seemed to win anything. In the nearly 50 years that the team has been around, they have only made the playoffs three times, all in the mid-1990s, and they have never won a playoff series. The Rangers tried unsuccessfully

to change their luck in 2001 by paying $252 million to sign superstar Alex Rodriguez for ten years. Problem was, that left no money to spend on pitching. Since 2001, the Rangers have never finished higher than eighteenth in major league team pitching, and have finished dead last three times. Rodriguez left for the Yankees in 2004, and the Rangers haven't been able to improve their record.

Texas Rangers

Founded in 1961
Other Names: Washington Senators
0 World Championships
0 AL pennants

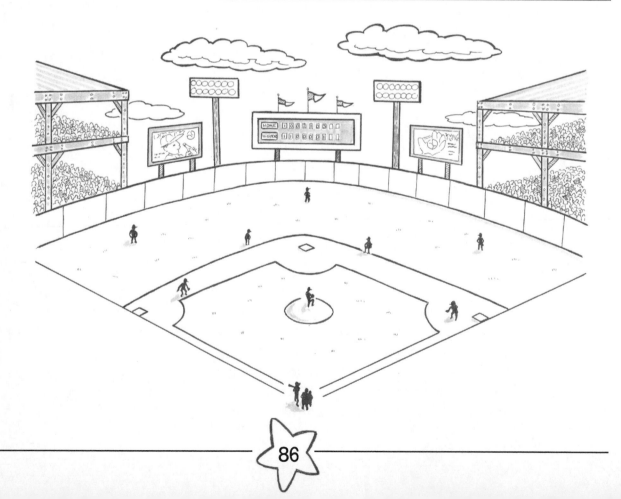

One of the great things about baseball is that on any given day anyone can be the big hero. It's fun to hear about people like Bucky Dent or Francisco Cabrera, who were never stars but happened to get a hit at an incredibly important time. But the best baseball players are the hitters who get important hits every couple of nights and the pitchers who are so good so often that no one wants to hit against them. These are today's stars who could be tomorrow's Hall-of-Famers.

Premier Pitchers

Twenty years ago, a starting pitcher was expected to pitch eight or nine innings. Nowadays, relief pitchers are used a lot more, and starters often pitch only five or six innings. That hasn't changed the fact that the most important player a team can have is an "ace" starter, someone you can rely on to shut down an opponent every time he takes the mound. Here are the best of the major league aces.

Johan Santana

Johan Santana, a two-time Cy Young Award winner, was born in Venezuela and signed a contract to play minor league baseball at age 16. He wasn't so great in his first major league season. The Twins sent him back to the minors to work on a changeup, which he mastered. Santana was an excellent relief pitcher for a couple of years before he began starting regularly, in 2004. Since then, he's thrown more than 200 innings every year, and his highest season ERA has been 3.33. In 2008 he left the Twins for the Mets; the National League hasn't had any more success hitting him than the American League did.

Johan Santana

W	ERA	K
122	3.12	1,733

Roy Halladay

Roy Halladay grew up in Denver and was drafted by the Blue Jays out of high school. His first season with Toronto was in 1998, and by 2001 he was a regular starting pitcher— and a good one. In 2003, he won the Cy Young Award. His 2005 season was even better—in 19 starts, he allowed less than one baserunner per inning, something almost unheard of for a starting pitcher. Unfortunately, a line drive broke his leg midseason, and he didn't pitch again until 2006. Since then he's been the Blue Jays' ace, finishing in the top five in Cy Young voting in every year. Halladay was traded to the Phillies before the 2010 season.

Roy Halladay

W	ERA	K
148	3.43	1,461

Tim Lincecum

Tim Lincecum led a state championship high school baseball team and then passed up minor league opportunities to play at the University of Washington. His only full year of minor league ball was 2006. In 2007, he struggled in his first major league starts. But by the end of the year he had found success. His pitching mechanics are excellent, and he has a blazing fast fastball. More importantly, his curveball can make batters look silly. He won the 2008 and 2009 Cy Young Award.

Save: When a pitcher comes into a close ballgame and gets the final outs, that pitcher earns a save.

OPS: One statistic that baseball people have learned to focus on is OPS, which stands for "on base percentage plus slugging percentage:" To calculate OPS, just add a player's on base percentage to his slugging percentage. A typical OPS is about .750. The best hitters have a season-long OPS above .900, and just a few each year make it above 1.000.

Tim Lincecum

W	ERA	K
40	2.90	676

Other Starting Pitchers

CC Sabathia helped the Brewers make the playoffs in 2008, then joined the Yankees. Cliff Lee, then with the Indians, led the AL in ERA in 2008, representing his first truly awesome year as a pitcher. He won 22 games on a team that only won 81 all season. Jake Peavy of the Padres has led the NL in ERA twice, and won the 2007 Cy Young Award. Lefty Cole Hamels of the Phillies was the ace of the staff that won the World Championship in 2008.

The Best Relievers

The best relievers in the game don't allow many base-runners at all. They can enter a game in a critical situation and get outs under pressure.

The Twins' Joe Nathan is one of the best. He came up as a starter with the Giants, but he converted to relief after a few years. He's made numerous all-star appearances with the Twins, and he's even earned many Cy Young votes—that's almost unheard of for a reliever.

Jonathan Papelbon of the Red Sox is a consistently strong reliever. You know every year he'll pitch about 60 innings and save about 40 games. He still hasn't given up a run in the postseason.

The Phillies' Brad Lidge was once an all-star with the Astros. But he gave up a game-winning homer to Albert Pujols in the playoffs back in 2005, and it seemed that his career was over. After two lousy years, the Phillies picked

WORDS to KNOW

Pitching Rotation: A starting pitcher can't pitch every day—his arm would get so sore it would fall off! Since games are scheduled almost every day, teams usually use a rotation of five pitchers who take turns starting.

him up, and all of a sudden he was good again—he was the best reliever on their 2008 World Championship team.

Top Hitters

A great hitter doesn't just hit lots of home runs. The best hitters get on base a lot, too. Pitchers certainly do not want to face any of these terrific hitters with the game on the line.

Albert Pujols

The Cardinals' first baseman has established himself as the most feared hitter in baseball. He can hit for power and for average; he rarely strikes out. In fact, he has walked more times than he has struck out. In 2003 Pujols became the youngest player ever to win a batting title. In 2004, he led the Cardinals to the World Series, and in 2006 he led them all the way to the World Championship. In 2008, when the Cardinals didn't make the playoffs, Pujols still led the league with a 1.114 OPS and won the NL MVP. And still, Pujols continues to work hard to improve his game. He is quite proud of his improved defense at first base.

Albert Pujols

HR	RBI	AVG
366	1,112	.334

Game Pieces

Baseball is such a familiar game that you might not even need words to describe it! Study the four picture puzzles below and see if you can figure out what baseball play, player, or place they each describe.

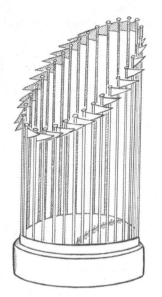

Alex Rodriguez

Through 15 seasons, A-Rod has already hit 553 home runs, including a career high 57 for Texas in 2002. He consistently scores more than 100 runs, drives in more than 100 runs, bats over .300 (.306 career), and averages about 20 steals per season. In 2001, the Texas Rangers offered him a record $25 million per season to leave the Mariners. In 2004, the Yankees bought out his contract, and Rodriguez began playing third base for them.

Alex Rodriguez

HR	RBI	AVG
583	1,706	.306

Manny Ramirez

No one in baseball is crazier than Manny, but boy, can he hit. In 2004, the Red Sox won their first World Series in 86 years behind Manny, the Series MVP. He earned the left field Silver Slugger—awarded to the best-hitting player at each position—eight times. In 2008, when he finished third in the majors with a 1.031 OPS, he left the Red Sox for the Dodgers and took them to the NLCS. Ramirez might be as well known for his terrible outfield play and his silliness off the field as for his incredible hitting. When Manny does something unusual, everyone says it's just "Manny being Manny." And his team is usually happy to let Manny be Manny while he drives in runs better than anyone else.

Manny Ramirez

HR	RBI	AVG
546	1,788	.313

WORDS to KNOW

MVP: MVP stands for Most Valuable Player. One player in each league wins the MVP award every year, not only for being a great player, but usually for helping their team go to the playoffs. The Baseball Writers' Association of America chooses who wins the MVP award.

Other Great Hitters

There are many other great hitters in baseball today—too many to name them all.

Houston first baseman Lance Berkman is a five-time all star who is among league leaders in every hitting stat every year.

Yankee first baseman and RBI machine Mark Teixeira had huge seasons with Texas, Atlanta, and Anaheim, which earned him big money with the Yankees.

Marlin Hanley Ramirez is a .300 hitter, hits for a .900 OPS, and also plays the most difficult infield position—shortstop.

Phillies second baseman Chase Utley has made the all-star team several years in a row, but he's probably prouder of the World Series that he and his team won in 2008.

All-Time Greats Who Are Still Playing

A few players who are nearing the end of their careers will almost surely be named to the Hall of Fame when they become eligible. Here they are, with stats as of the end of the 2009 season.

Chipper Jones

In his first full year, 1995, the Braves' new third baseman helped the team win the World Championship. Since then, Chipper has been a team leader and the Braves' most consistent hitter. He won the NL MVP award in 1999. As he's gotten older, he's lost time to injury, but his hitting has never stopped being awesome. In 2008, at age 36, his 1.044 OPS was second-best in the majors! Partially because the Braves

were in the playoffs for so many years, Chipper ranks with the best postseason players ever.

Chipper Jones

HR	RBI	AVG
426	1,445	.307

Derek Jeter

The Yankees' shortstop is also their captain, the undisputed leader of a team that has made the postseason nearly every year since 1995. The highlight of his career is his game-winning home run in extra innings at Yankee Stadium in Game 4 of the 2001 World Series. But the highlights that define Jeter's play are a result of his defensive hustle. Opposing teams get sick of seeing video clips of Jeter picking up a ground ball deep in the hole, throwing off balance, and robbing the batter of a hit. In an AL division series against the Oakland A's, Jeter came out of nowhere to catch an errant throw from an outfielder, nailing an Oakland runner at home and saving the series for the Yankees. In a 2004 game against the arch-rival Red Sox, he dived into the stands to catch a foul pop in extra innings, bloodying his chin but helping earn an eventual Yankees win. Jeter is one of New York City's most adored celebrities in addition to being the Yankees' most consistent player.

Derek Jeter

HR	RBI	AVG
224	1,068	.317

FUN FACT

Classic Game

For more than 40 years, Strat-O-Matic (*www.strat-o-matic.com*) has been making the ideal baseball board game. You can select your favorite team from the past season or pick up some classic teams from years gone by. There is a computerized version, but the standard version with cards and dice is still as wonderful as ever.

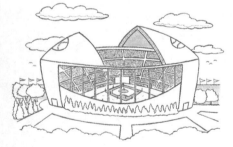

Mariano Rivera

Rivera pitched in his fifteenth season with the Yankees in 2009. He has been the rock of the Yankees bullpen through their years of dominance. Rivera has pitched in the postseason in every year of his career except one, compiling an incredible postseason ERA of 0.77. Think about it—in the postseason, he was pitching only against the best teams in the MLB. He has pitched 117 postseason innings, which is much more than a full regular season's worth of relief work. And in those 117 innings, he has allowed—get this—only 10 earned runs. Some pitchers give that up in two games!

Mariano Rivera

Saves	ERA	K
482	2.29	934

Ken Griffey Jr.

For a long time, people just called him "Junior," because his dad was also named Ken Griffey and was a great player for the Reds. In fact, when Griffey joined the majors in 1989, he played on the Seattle Mariners with his dad—the only time that's ever happened. Griffey, who genuinely loves to play the game, is one of the greatest center fielders ever, making many amazing catches and winning the Gold Glove for defense every year. He is a major home run threat as well, often compared to the great Willie Mays. Griffey hit 56 home runs in 1997 and again in 1998, and he had more than 140 RBIs each year. In 2000, he joined the Cincinnati Reds, the team on which his dad became famous. Unfortunately, injury after injury has slowed Junior down. He hit his 500th home run in 2004; Griffey was fifth on the all-time home

Larry!

Chipper Jones earned his nickname from his family because he seemed like a "chip off the old block," meaning that he was a lot like his dad. His real first name is Larry. In the 1999 NLCS, Mets fans made fun of Chipper by shouting, "Lar-ry! Lar-ry!"

FUN FACT

Baseball Hangman

In baseball hangman, you choose major league players or teams for your game. Put down blank spaces for the letters in the name you choose, and let your opponent guess the letters as you draw the hangman or fill in the correct letters.

run list at the beginning of the 2009 season, and he still has a chance to catch Mays for fourth.

Ken Griffey Jr.

HR	RBI	AVG
630	1,829	.285

Griffey's stats are as of the end of the 2009 season.

FUN FACT

Not the Yankees

Do you know which team has the most players in the Hall of Fame? It's not the Yankees; it's the Giants, who have 24 Hall-of-Famers.

The Baseball Hall of Fame

In 1936, the baseball community decided that they needed a place to honor the greatest players ever. In June 1939, the National Baseball Hall of Fame and Museum was opened in Cooperstown, New York. It's a place where you'll find bats and gloves used by the greatest players, balls that were hit for historic home runs, and plenty of other neat baseball stuff. The Hall includes plaques honoring the 260 members, which include 195 major-league players along with managers and other people closely associated with the game. There are even eight umpires included.

Cooperstown

How to Make It into the Hall of Fame

Making the Hall of Fame is a tremendous honor that only a small number of baseball players ever receive. A player must be retired from baseball for five years before he is eligible to be elected to the Hall. Most players are voted in by baseball writers—writers can vote for up to ten players on each year's ballot. A player who receives votes from three-fourths of the writers becomes a Hall-of-Famer. Generally, only two or so players make the Hall of Fame each year.

There is a lot to see, including films and even an actual ball field where two major-league teams square off every summer in a special exhibition game. The Hall of Fame also has special programs that include movies and "sandlot stories" about the game. There are also book signings by some of the many authors who write about the game, which often include former players, managers, and popular broadcasters. There's even a daily scavenger hunt for kids to take part in during the summer months. You may have to move through the Hall of Fame slowly because (a) it's crowded, and (b) there's so much to check out!

A Little History of the Hall

The idea for the Hall of Fame began in Cooperstown in the 1930s. Cooperstown was where Abner Doubleday, who many credit with inventing the game, had lived, so it seemed to be the ideal place to build such a museum to honor the game. In 1936, as baseball approached its 100th anniversary, plans were made to honor the greatest players of the game. That year, the first five players—Ty Cobb, Babe Ruth, Honus Wagner, Christy Mathewson, and Walter Johnson—were voted in as the first players to make the Hall of Fame.

By 1939, the actual building was completed. There was a big ceremony that summer, and the Hall of Fame was officially opened, displaying all sorts of stuff from the game. It was a small museum at first, but thousands of people flocked to tiny Cooperstown to visit. Over the years the Hall has grown, with new wings added on to accommodate all of the new exhibits plus a gallery, a library, and more. Today, between 300,000 and 400,000 people visit the baseball shrine annually. That's quite a lot of visitors for a town whose population is only 2,300 people.

FUN FACT

Baseball on TV

Baseball has figured in the plot or back-story of lots of television shows. On the old comedy *Cheers*, Sam used to be a pitcher for the Boston Red Sox. On *Seinfeld*, George worked for Yankees owner George Steinbrenner. But perhaps the most famous baseball TV show ever was the episode of *The Simpsons* in which nine major-league players decided to play for Mr. Burns's power plant softball team alongside Homer.

How do you get to the Baseball Hall of Fame?

To find the answer, follow the correct path from PLAY BALL to GAME OVER. Collect the letters along the way, and write them in order on the lines below.

_ _ _ _ _ _ _ / _ _ _ _ _ _ / _ _ _ _ _ _ !

Chapter 6
The World Series

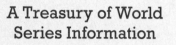
"The Fall Classic," as the World Series is often called, is the peak of the baseball season, when the best in the American League and the best in the National League square off for the championship of Major League baseball. Many of baseball's greatest players have performed at their best in the Series; many of baseball's most memorable moments have occurred during the Series. But the World Series is more than a simple means of crowning a champion. It is a national event, a yearly cultural milepost that guides the memories of many Americans.

A Treasury of World Series Information

The website *www.baseball-almanac.com* includes detailed summaries of every World Series, including box scores from each game.

Origins of the World Series

The World Series began in 1903, when the National League and the American League agreed to compete to crown an overall champion. Until 1969, the American and National League teams never met until the World Series. There were no playoffs, and there were only eight teams in each league. The team that won the most games in the season won their league's pennant; the two pennant winners would then play the World Series, which started right after the end of the season. In 1969, when the leagues went to twelve teams each, they were divided into two divisions of six teams each, labeled East and West. The East and West champions played a playoff series to decide who would go to the World Series. Now there are thirty major-league teams and three divisions in each league (East, Central, and West), plus two rounds of playoffs. But no matter how they get there, the pennant-winning teams in each league meet in the World Series.

The Yankees have appeared in far more World Series and won more championships than any other team. Between 1927 and 1964 the Yankees were almost always in the Series. As the 1900s came to an end, the Yankees put their

Subway Series: In New York City, most people get from place to place via the subway. When two New York teams play each other in the Series, it's called a "Subway Series." The most recent Subway Series was in 2000, when the Yankees beat the Mets.

stamp on the World Series by winning titles in 1996, 1998, 1999, and 2000, giving them twenty-six titles overall.

Over a Century of the World Series

Many of baseball's most memorable moments occurred in World Series games. Here are some highlights of notable World Series events.

1903: On September 16, the first World Series ever began. It pitted the Pittsburgh Pirates against the Boston Americans (who became the Boston Red Sox in 1908). The Americans won the Series five games to three. Cy Young won two games.

1904: The World Series was not played, because the NL champion New York Giants refused to play the AL champion Boston Americans. The Giants said the American League wasn't good enough to play with them. (That's funny, since Boston's American League team had beaten the NL's Pirates the previous year.)

1905: The New York Giants beat the Philadelphia A's four games to one. All five games were shutouts. Christy Mathewson pitched an incredible three complete game shutouts and walked only one batter for the most amazing overall pitching performance in World Series history.

1908: The Chicago Cubs beat the Detroit Tigers four games to one to win their second title in a row. The Cubs have not won a World Series since.

1918: Babe Ruth won two games as a pitcher and the Red Sox won their third World Series in four years, beating the Cubs four games to two. They didn't win another Series for 86 years.

1919: This year's White Sox team became known as the Black Sox after they lost the Series to the Reds, five games

Best of Seven

The World Series is played as a best-of-seven series: this means that the first team to win four games wins the Series, and there can't be more than seven games. In 1903, and again in 1918 through 1920, the Series was played as best of nine, but it was changed back to today's best-of-seven format.

Perfect Game

A pitcher pitches a perfect game when he gets every batter out for a whole game. That's only happened 17 times in the major leagues—and only once in the World Series.

to three, and were accused of losing the Series on purpose because they were paid money by gamblers. Eight White Sox players were banned from baseball for life. The White Sox did not win another Series until 2005.

1921: The Giants beat the Yankees five games to three in the first ever all–New York Series.

1936: The Yankees scored 18 runs in Game 2 and 13 runs in Game 6 en route to a 4–2 Series win over their across-the-river rivals, the Giants. It was the Yankees' first post-Ruth World Series and featured Lou Gehrig and Joe DiMaggio together for the first time in the postseason.

1944: The first and only all–St. Louis World Series featured the Browns against the Cardinals. The two teams scored a low total of 28 runs in the entire six-game series, which the Cardinals won, four games to two.

1954: In a 2–2 opening game between the Giants and the Indians, Willie Mays made what may be baseball's most famous catch, running to the deepest part of center field and grabbing the ball with his back to home plate to keep the score tied. The Giants won the Series 4–0.

1955: After losing five times to the Yankees in the World Series, the Brooklyn Dodgers finally defeated them four games to three to win their only World Championship. Duke Snider hit four homers and Johnny Podres pitched two complete game victories, including a Game 7 shutout.

1956: In Game 5, Don Larsen of the Yankees pitched the only perfect World Series game ever. The Yankees won the Series over the Dodgers once again, this time in seven games, 4–3.

1960: Second baseman Bill Mazeroski hit a walk-off home run in the bottom of the ninth inning of the seventh game to give the underdog Pirates a win over the mighty Yankees.

Lots of Games

Catcher Yogi Berra of the Yankees played 75 World Series games—more than anyone else ever has.

walk-off home run: When a player on the home team hits a home run in the bottom of the last inning to win the game, that player's team can walk off the field after the runs score. The game is over, regardless of how many outs are left, because the opposing team won't have a chance to score.

The "Whole World" Series

While the World Series is played here in America, baseball is popular all over the world! See if you can match the country names with their location to fill in the grid. We left you the W-O-R-L-D S-E-R-I-E-S to help.

TOGO MEXICO
PERU ITALY
EGYPT TAIWAN
IRAN CANADA
COOK ISLANDS
PUERTO RICO
RUSSIA

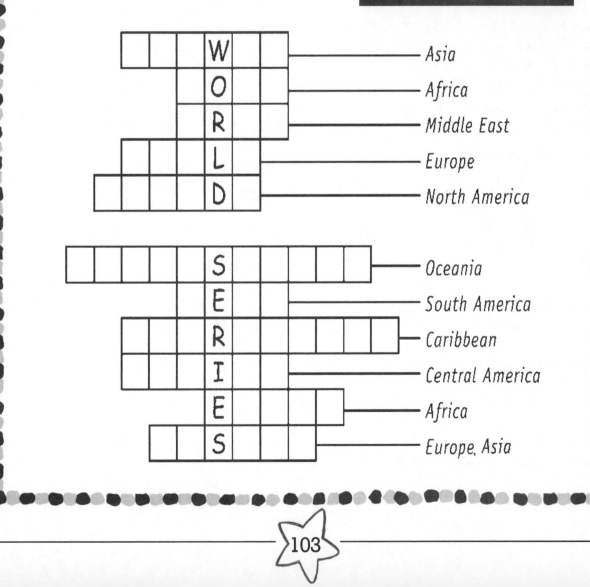

— Asia
— Africa
— Middle East
— Europe
— North America

— Oceania
— South America
— Caribbean
— Central America
— Africa
— Europe, Asia

FUN FACT

Bucky Dent

The Yankees and the Red Sox ended the 1978 season tied for first place in the American League East. They played one game to decide which team went to the playoffs. The Yankees shortstop, Bucky Dent, hit only five home runs all season. But he hit the biggest homer of his career to win the game for the Yankees and extend the Curse of the Bambino.

Seven Wins

Cardinals pitcher Bob Gibson won seven World Series games, even though his team made only three trips to the Series. In one game he struck out 17 batters.

1966: An amazing Orioles pitching staff shut the Dodgers out three consecutive times, including two 1–0 games, to complete a four-game sweep. The Dodgers had only two runs on seventeen hits.

1969: The Mets—the team known as the worst in baseball for their first seven years—came from nowhere to win 100 games in the regular season. Then they beat the favored Orioles 4–1 in the Series. Game 3 featured two amazing diving catches by Mets outfielder Tommie Agee.

1975: In the bottom of the twelfth inning of Game 6, Red Sox Hall of Fame catcher Carleton Fisk hit a home run over Fenway Park's Green Monster to win the game and force a Game 7. The famous replay shows Fisk jogging down the first base line, trying to "push" his home run fair. The Reds won the seventh game and the Series, 4–3. Five games were decided by one run in this very close Series.

1977: Reggie Jackson hit three consecutive home runs in the sixth game to lead the Yankees to a 4–2 Series win over the Dodgers. Jackson hit five home runs and batted .450 in the Series. Based on this and other outstanding postseason performances, Reggie Jackson became known as "Mr. October."

1980: Tug McGraw struck out batters with the bases loaded in Games 5 and 6 to secure two wins for the Phillies, who won their first World Series. Hall-of-Famers Steve Carlton and Mike Schmidt were Phillies heroes.

1986: After being down to their final out in Game 6, the Mets rallied in the tenth inning to beat the Red Sox when Mookie Wilson hit a ground ball through first baseman Bill Buckner's legs, scoring Ray Knight to force a seventh game. The Mets blew out the Sox in Game 7 to win the Series.

1988: An injured Kirk Gibson pinch hit a dramatic two-run walk-off homer to win the first game of the Series

for the Dodgers over the favored Oakland A's. The homer started the Dodgers off on the way to a 4–1 Series win.

1989: This year's World Series pitted the Oakland A's against the San Francisco Giants. Less than an hour before Game 2 was to begin, a terrible earthquake hit the area, causing all kinds of damage. Game 2 was postponed, but a week later, the cities and the MLB decided to continue with the Series. The A's beat the Giants 4–0 in the Earthquake Series.

1993: For only the second time in World Series history, the Series ended on a game-winning home run. This homer came off the bat of Toronto Blue Jay's slugger Joe Carter, who gave the Jays an 8–6 win in the sixth and final game.

1995: The Atlanta Braves won thirteen straight division titles between 1991 and 2004, making it to the World Series five times. But the Braves won only one championship, in 1995, when they beat the Indians in six games.

1999: The Yankees won their third title in four years and secured their place as team of the decade, beating the Braves 4–0. It was the fourth time in seven years the Braves lost the World Series.

2001: The World Series between the Arizona Diamondbacks and the New York Yankees started a week later than planned because baseball took a week off after the attacks on the World Trade Center and the Pentagon in September. The country suddenly was at war, yet baseball continued.

Games 3, 4, and 5 were played at Yankee Stadium below a torn flag pulled from the wreckage of the World Trade Center, and President George W. Bush was on hand. The Yankees twice pulled off improbable comeback victories: In Game 4, first baseman Tino Martinez hit a homer in the bottom of the ninth to tie the game, and then shortstop Derek Jeter hit the game-winning homer in the bottom of the tenth. In Game 5, third baseman Scott Brosius hit a walk-off

FUN FACT

The Closer

Yankee relief pitcher John Wetteland became the first pitcher ever to save all four wins for his team in the 1996 World Series against Atlanta.

FUN FACT

Marathon Match-Ups

Games 3 and 4 of the 2004 ALCS were two of the longest playoff games in history. The Yankees and the Red Sox played almost eleven hours of baseball in two days! But neither game holds the record for longest playoff game. In 2005, the Astros beat the Braves after an exhilarating eighteen-inning game that ran for five hours and fifty minutes.

home run in the bottom of the ninth to send the series back to Arizona. The Diamondbacks won Game 6 in a blowout; then they rallied in the bottom of the ninth in Game 7 to win on a bloop RBI single by Luis Gonzalez.

2002: The San Francisco Giants led the Anaheim Angels three games to two. In Game 6 the Giants were ahead 5–0 in the seventh inning, but the Angels came back to win, 6–5. In Game 7, the Angels took an early 4–1 lead and coasted from there to the championship.

2003: The Yankees once again represented the American League in the Series, but this time their veteran pitching couldn't top the Florida Marlins' young starters. The Marlins triumphed in six games, the last a complete game shutout by Josh Beckett.

2004: The Boston Red Sox broke the Curse of the Bambino, winning their first World Series since 1918. The World Series itself, in which Boston swept the St. Louis Cardinals 4–0, was almost anticlimactic after both League Championship Series. In the National League, the Cardinals, led by superstar Albert Pujols, beat the Houston Astros and 40-year-old Roger Clemens in an intense seven-game series.

But the American League Championship Series, a reprise of the 2003 Yankees vs. Red Sox battle, captured most of the country's attention. The Yankees took a 3–0 lead in the series; no team in baseball history had ever come back to win a best-of-seven series after being down 3–0. But the Red Sox did it. They won two games in extra innings, each ending well after midnight. Curt Schilling pitched two games, even though one of his ankles was so injured that it bled visibly during the game. The Sox put away Game 7 early, taking an insurmountable lead on Mark Bellhorn's grand slam home run. The Sox kept their momentum and steamrolled the power-hitting Cardinals in four games, capping the most exciting postseason in recent history.

Name Change

In 1919, the Chicago White Sox were accused of being paid to lose the World Series! After that, the team became known by another name. Fill in all the letters that are not W-H-I-T-E to find out what it was.

BWLHAICTKESOX

2005: Game 3 of the White Sox–Astros series turned into a marathon. In the middle of the night, way past even your parents' bedtime, Geoff Blum of the White Sox hit a fourteenth-inning home run that stood up for the win. The White Sox finished their sweep of the Astros the next night, when series MVP Jermaine Dye drove in the only run of the game with an eighth-inning single.

2006: Just three years before, the Detroit Tigers had been the laughing stock of baseball, finishing with the second-worst season record ever. But in 2006, their talented young pitching staff dominated American League opposition. It seemed like the Tigers were on a roll to the championship. Their NL opponent was the St. Louis Cardinals, who

FUN FACT

Hard Luck Teams

Through most of your lifetime, even through your parents and grandparents' lifetimes, major-league baseball has told the story of three hard-luck teams: the Red Sox, the White Sox, and the Cubs. These teams had been good back in the 1900s and 1910s, but hadn't won a championship since then. All of a sudden, though, luck seems to have changed: the Red Sox won in 2004 and 2007; the White Sox won in 2005. Could the Cubs be next?

squeaked into the postseason with a weak record in a weak division. Aside from superstar Albert Pujols and former Cy Young winner Chris Carpenter, the Cardinals seemed more gritty than good.

In the World Series, though, it was the Cardinals who dominated. MVP shortstop David Eckstein, whom many thought was too small and weak-armed to play in the majors, not only hit .364 but also anchored a solid defense that led the team to victory. Pitcher Jeff Weaver, who had been released earlier in the year for poor performance, made two solid starts and was the winning pitcher in the decisive Game 5. It helped the Cardinals that the Tigers' defense made eight errors in five games.

2007: A stacked Red Sox team dominated the Colorado Rockies to sweep their way to Boston's second title of the young century. The Sox were challenged in the ALCS by the Indians, who took a 3–1 lead, but they won their last seven postseason games behind the pitching of Josh Beckett and the suddenly amazing bat of J.D. Drew. The Rockies were not an unworthy opponent. In perhaps the most incredible regular season finish ever, they went 14–1 over the season's last few weeks just to make the playoffs. Then, the Rockies swept the division series and the NLCS. But their luck ran out when they went up against the Red Sox, who proved themselves to be one of the best baseball teams in existence.

2008: Not only were the 2008 Rays the first winning team in franchise history, they won their division and went all the way to the Series. But then they ran into the Phillies. The teams split two close games in Florida, then went to cold and rainy Philadelphia. Game 3 was delayed by an hour and a half. In Game 5, Philly led when a huge rainstorm hit. If the umpires had called the game, the rules would have declared the Phillies the winners, without giving the Rays

the chance to come back. Finally, despite the puddles on the field and the downpour, the Rays tied the game. This allowed the umpires to suspend the game to finish another time. Two days later, the Phillies took the lead and won both the game and the Series.

2009: Every year, the Yankees pay more money for players than anyone else. Yet the Bronx Bombers got to the World Series in 2009 for only the second time in the decade. A big reason for their success was that third baseman Alex Rodriguez, the highest paid player in baseball, finally lived up to his potential in the postseason. Rodriguez's six homers and 18 RBI in the playoffs, combined with World Series MVP Hideki Matsui's 13 RBI and closer Mariano Rivera's 16 strong innings, took the Yanks to their 27th World Championship, this time over the Phillies.

Chapter 7
Statistics and Records

More than any other sport, statistics are very much a part of baseball. Since the beginning of the sport, fans have wanted to know who had the most hits, who made the error, who got the win, and so on. Home run totals, batting averages, wins, strikeouts—they are all a central part of baseball's popularity. Sometimes when a player was on the verge of breaking a record, like when Cal Ripken Jr. played in his 2,131st game, or when Hank Aaron hit home run number 715, the individual achievements of the players got more attention than the ballgame. That's part of what makes baseball so interesting. Your team may not be doing well, like the Giants in 2006, but you might want to watch them to see a slugger like Barry Bonds pile up home runs on his way to a record.

There's a stat for everything in baseball. You could probably find the answer to "What pitcher threw the most wild pitches in night games at Wrigley Field in the 1940s?" Okay, so that's a trick question—there were no night games at Wrigley in the 1940s because they had no lights. But the point is that if you love statistics you could probably spend a year looking at baseball statistics and never see the same one twice.

Individual Stats

Players' individual statistics, or "stats," are followed closely, not only by fans but also by sportswriters, team management, and everyone associated with baseball. There are actually thousands of statistics that are recorded, from how long it took to play a game to how many times a hitter grounded out to the shortstop. Many baseball stats, such as batting average or runs batted in, have been kept and published since the late 19th and early 20th centuries. Others, like saves and holds, have been devised in more recent

FUN FACT

Back-to-Back No-Hitters!

The only pitcher ever to throw no-hitters in two starts in a row was Johnny Vander Meer of the Cincinnati Reds in 1938.

years. Computers have made it easy to quickly calculate somewhat more obscure statistics, such as slugging percentage or batting average with runners in scoring position. The following are the most common player statistics you will see in the sports pages. Statistics for each game are usually found in what was termed back in the 1800s as a "box score," or a summary of the game in a box. More than 100 years later, whether you find box scores in the newspaper or online, they are still the most popular way to see what happened in a ballgame.

Box Score

On Saturday, October 2, 2004, the Dodgers and the Giants were fighting for first place in the NL East and a playoff spot. The Dodgers trailed 3–0 entering the ninth inning; but they came back to win, the decisive runs coming on Steve Finley's walk-off grand slam home run. This victory clinched the division title for the Dodgers.

Box Scores

Team	1 2 3	4 5 6	7 8 9	R H E
San Francisco Giants	0 0 0	2 0 0	1 0 0	3 6 2
Los Angeles Dodgers	0 0 0	0 0 0	0 0 7	7 7 0

Giants Dodgers

NAME	Pos	ab	r	h	rbi	bb	so	avg
Durham	2b	5	0	1	0	0	1	.280
Izturis	ss	5	1	0	1	0	0	.288
Tucker	rf	4	0	0	0	1	1	.256
Werth	lf	5	1	2	1	0	1	.266
Alfonzo	3b	4	0	1	0	0	1	.289

Giants Dodgers

NAME	Pos	ab	r	h	rbi	bb	so	avg
Finley	cf	5	1	2	4	0	0	.271
Snow	1b	4	1	2	0	0	1	.327
Beltre	3b	4	0	0	0	0	0	.335
Cruz	ss	4	0	0	0	0	0	.293
Green	rf	4	1	2	0	0	0	.266
Ransom	ss	0	0	0	0	0	0	.258
Ventura	1b	3	1	0	0	1	2	.243
Pierzynski	c	3	0	0	0	1	1	.270
Cora	2b	2	0	0	0	2	1	.264
Hermanson	p	0	0	0	0	0	0	.100
Mayne	c	2	0	0	0	0	0	.221
Christiansen	p	0	0	0	0	0	0	.000
Grabowski	ph	1	0	0	0	0	1	.219
Herges	p	0	0	0	0	0	0	.000
Ross	c	0	0	0	0	0	0	.172
Franklin	p	0	0	0	0	0	0	.333
Hernandez	ph	0	1	0	0	1	0	.287
Grissom	cf	3	1	2	3	1	0	.277
Dessens	p	1	0	0	0	0	0	.182
Tomko	p	3	0	0	0	1	2	.113
Alvarez	p	1	0	0	0	0	0	.161
Eyre	p	0	0	0	0	0	0	.000
Sanchez	p	0	0	0	0	0	0	.250
Torrealba	c	0	0	0	0	0	0	.228
Venafro	p	0	0	0	0	0	0	.000
Carrara	p	0	0	0	0	0	0	.000
Saenz	ph	1	0	1	0	0	0	.282
Flores	pr	0	0	0	0	0	0	.000
Brazoban	p	0	0	0	0	0	0	.000

Giants Dodgers

NAME	Pos	ab	r	h	rbi	bb	so	avg
Choi	ph	0	0	0	1	1	0	.253
Perez	pr	0	1	0	0	0	0	.300
Totals		31	3	6	3	6	5	
Totals		34	7	7	7	5	5	

E—Grissom, Ransom. LOB—San Francisco 8, Los Angeles 7.
GIDP—Pierzynski. HR—Grissom (21), Finley (36). S—Torrealba.

Pitchers

NAME	ip	h	r	er	bb	so	era
Tomko	7.1	4	0	0	2	4	4.04
Dessens	4	3	2	2	3	3	4.46
Eyre	0.1	0	0	0	0	0	4.10
Alvarez	2	0	0	0	1	0	4.03
Hermanson (L, 6–9)	0.2	1	4	4	3	1	4.53
Sanchez	0.1	2	1	1	0	1	3.38
Christiansen	0	0	1	0	0	0	4.50
Venafro	.01	0	0	0	0	0	4.00
Herges	0	1	1	1	0	0	5.23
Carrara	1.1	1	0	0	1	1	2.18
Franklin	0	1	1	1	0	0	6.39
Brazoban (W, 6–2)	1	0	0	0	1	0	2.48

Umpires: HP—McClelland, 1b—Randazzo, 2b—Culbreth, 3b—Wolf. Time of game: 3:40. Attendance: 46,005

R, H, and E are runs, hits, and errors for each team for the game.

The rest of the abbreviations are as follows:

Pos is the position that player played. Sometimes a backup will take over at that position, like on the Giants' side where you see Cruz at shortstop (ss) replaced by Ransom.

You may wonder what this all means. Well, it's very simple once you learn about the format.

Across the top is the inning-by-inning account of runs scored. You'll see that the Giants got 2 in the top of the fourth and another in the top of the seventh inning, but the Dodgers got 7 in the bottom of the ninth.

The positions are:

1b	First base
2b	Second base
3b	Third base
ss	Shortstop
lf	Left fielder
cf	Center fielder
rf	Right fielder
c	Catcher
p	Pitcher
ph	Pinch hitter (someone who bats for another player, such as Saenz or Choi in the game above)
pr	Pinch runner (someone who runs for someone else, such as Florez in the game above)
dh	In the American League and in some minor leagues there are designated hitters, who bat for the pitchers.

The rest of the stats tell you what each player did in the game.

FUN FACT

The Ultimate Inning

In 1999, Fernando Tatis of the St. Louis Cardinals hit a grand slam home run. His team kept on hitting and scoring runs in the inning, so he got to bat again in the same inning with the bases loaded. Believe it or not, he hit another grand slam, becoming the first player ever to hit two grand slam home runs and drive in eight runs in one inning. Wow!

WORDS to KNOW

batting average: A player's batting average is a good measure of his ability to hit. The best hitters have a .300 average or better. A player hitting .200 might be sent back to the minor leagues; no one has hit .400 for an entire season since Ted Williams hit .406 in 1941. To calculate a batting average, divide a player's hits by his at bats.

ab	At bats, or how many times the batter officially had a turn at bat (walks, sacrifices, and being hit by a pitch don't count as official at bats)
r	Runs scored
h	Hits
rbi	Runs batted in (a hit or another play that brings in a run or more)
bb	Base on balls (or walks)
so	Strikeouts, also sometimes listed as "k"
avg	Batting average

There will also be some information listed underneath the line that says "totals," telling you who hit doubles (2B), triples (3B), and home runs (HR) and how many of each the player has for the season. You'll also see if a player had a sacrifice (S) or a sacrifice fly (SF), or if he grounded into a double play (GIDP). Players don't like to see it, but there is also a listing of errors (E) as well. Stolen bases (SB) and caught stealing (CS) are listed next. Some box scores may give you more detailed information, but these are the basics.

Pitching statistics are also included. You'll often find next to pitchers' names the "decision," meaning the win (W) or loss (L), or the save (S) for a reliever. In the game above, Brazoban was the winning pitcher in relief of Dessens, and no save was credited. Hermanson was the losing pitcher, also in relief. His win-loss record is listed as 6–9, or six wins and nine losses for the season.

Other numbers you may see next to the name are:

bs   Blown saves, which tell you how many the pitcher has blown.

h   Hold, an unofficial statistic, will show up for relief pitchers. It means they held the lead until the closer came in and finished the game.

Then you'll see what is called the "pitcher's line" for the game, which includes:

ip   Innings pitched. Sometimes you'll see a decimal like 7.1, meaning the pitcher lasted seven innings and got one out in the eighth. 7.2 would mean he got two outs in the eighth.

h   Hits allowed

r   Runs allowed

er   Earned runs allowed. Not all runs count as "earned runs." If an error on a play put a future scorer on base or helped a runner to score, that run does not count toward a pitcher's ERA. In the game above the errors didn't allow any runs to score, so all runs were earned.

bb   Base on balls, or walks allowed

so   Strikeouts (sometimes listed as "k")

era   The up-to-date earned run average of the pitcher, or how many earned runs he allows per nine innings. Pitchers try to keep their ERAs under 4.00, which is getting harder to do. Starting pitchers pitch more innings, so it's harder for them to keep those ERAs down. An ERA under 3.50 is quite good; under 3.00 is excellent.

Now check out the newspaper or your favorite online sports site to find more box scores. Even if you didn't watch or listen to the game, you can figure out what happened or what your favorite player did. Reading box scores is the best way to keep up with what's happening in major-league baseball.

FUN FACT

I'll Play Anywhere

Only two players in baseball history have played all ten positions. That's right, ten . . . Bert Campaneris of the A's and Cesar Tovar of the Twins not only played all nine defensive positions, including one pitching appearance each, but they were also designated hitters.

WORDS to KNOW

sacrifice: When a batter bunts, allowing himself to be thrown out but advancing runners, he is credited with a sacrifice. A sacrifice does not count as a time at bat.

Shutouts

A pitcher earns a shutout by holding the opposing team without a run for the whole game. The pitcher who threw the most shutouts in baseball history was Walter Johnson, "the Big Train," who blanked the other team 110 times in his career.

fielding percentage: One measure of a fielder's strength is the fielding percentage. To calculate this stat, add the player's putouts and assists. Then, divide by the total of the player's putouts, assists, and errors. A good fielder will have a fielding percentage of .980 or .990. Outfielders are expected to have higher fielding percentages than infielders.

Player Statistics

If you look up a player on the Internet or in a baseball book (including this one), you'll find ballplayers' statistics for each season and for their careers.

The most commonly found stats for hitters include:

G	Games played
AB	At bats
R	Runs
H	Hits
2B	Doubles
3B	Triples
HR	Home runs
RBI	Runs batted in
BB	Base on balls (also known as walks)
K or SO	Strikeouts
AVG	Batting average
SB	Stolen bases
CS	Caught stealing

You might also see SLG, or slugging percentage, which takes one point for each single, two for each double, three for each triple, and four for each home run, adds them up and divides by the number of at bats. Unlike batting averages, which rarely top .350, slugging percentages for the best power hitters can reach .600 or higher.

Common pitching stats include:

W   Wins

L   Losses

PCT   Winning percentage, or how often the pitcher gets a win versus a loss. Add together wins and losses, then take the number of wins and divide it by the number you get. For example, if a pitcher has a win-loss record of 10 wins and 2 losses, you would add 10 + 2 = 12. Then divide the 10 wins by 12 and you'll get .833.

G   Games pitched in

GS   Games started

CG   Complete games

Sho   Shutouts (held the opposing team to no runs)

IP   Innings pitched

Hits   Hits allowed

BB   Base on balls allowed

K or SO Strikeouts

ERA   Earned run average

And for relief pitchers the two most common stats are:

S   Saves

BS   Blown saves

The same statistics listed for a player can also be found for a team. The stats listed here are the basics, but you can find more in books that go into greater detail.

WORDS to KNOW

ERA: ERA stands for a pitcher's earned run average, or how many runs that pitcher is likely to give up in a full nine-inning game. To calculate ERA, multiply the number of earned runs allowed by 9; then divide by the number of innings pitched.

assist: When a player makes a throw of any kind to get an out, whether it's an infielder throwing a batter out at first base or an outfielder throwing out a runner at home plate, the fielder gets credit for an assist.

putout: The fielder who steps on the base or applies a tag to actually put the runner out gets credit for a putout.

Lucky Numbers

Baseball is a game full of numbers. There's the RBI and ERA numbers, the numbers on the scoreboard, and of course the lucky number on the shirt of your favorite player!

In this tricky little puzzle, you must figure out what lucky combination of numbers to use so that each column (up and down) or row (across) adds up to the right totals shown in the white numbers. The white arrows show you in which direction you will be adding. Lucky you—four numbers are in place to get you started!

Here are the rules:

- You are only adding the numbers in any set of white boxes that are touching each other.
- Use only the numbers 1 through 9. Each number can only be used *once* in each set.
- Remember that each answer has to be correct both across *and* down!

Statistics and Records

The Standings

To follow your favorite team, you can look in the newspaper at the sports pages or on a website like *www.baseball-reference.com* to get plenty of information including the standings and the listings of who's in first place, second place, and so on.

The major leagues today are each broken into three divisions:

American League

East	Central	West
Baltimore Orioles	Chicago White Sox	Anaheim Angels
Boston Red Sox	Cleveland Indians	Oakland Athletics
New York Yankees	Detroit Tigers	Seattle Mariners
Tampa Bay Rays	Kansas City Royals	Texas Rangers
Toronto Blue Jays	Minnesota Twins	

National League

East	Central	West
Atlanta Braves	Chicago Cubs	Arizona Diamondbacks
Florida Marlins	Cincinnati Reds	Colorado Rockies
Washington Nationals	Houston Astros	Los Angeles Dodgers
New York Mets	Milwaukee Brewers	San Diego Padres
Philadelphia Phillies	Pittsburgh Pirates	San Francisco Giants
	St. Louis Cardinals	

Other Columns You May See in the Standings Chart

- **Division:** the team's record against teams in their own division
- **Home/Road:** the team's record when playing at their home park, and the team's record when playing away from home

- **Interleague:** the team's record in games against the other league
- **Streak:** how many games the team has won or lost in a row
- **Last 10:** the team's record in their last 10 games

When you look at the standings in the papers, you'll see how many wins and losses the team has and their winning percentage, meaning what percentage of all the games they've played that they've won.

Games Behind

When you look at the standings, you will also see the abbreviation "GB" (games behind), which is a way of judging how close your team is to first place in their division. Games behind means how many times your team would have to beat the first place team in order to catch up with them. You might see:

Team	W–L	GB
New York Yankees	60–40	——
Boston Red Sox	58–42	2
Baltimore Orioles	54–48	7
Toronto Blue Jays	49–50	?
Tampa Bay Rays	40–60	?

How do you figure this out?

You subtract how many games the teams are apart in wins and then do the same for losses. In the first example, you can figure out the difference between the Yankees and Red Sox.

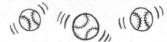
In wins you have 60 – 58 = 2.

In losses you have 42 – 40 = 2.

Then add the two numbers you came up with together: 2 + 2 = 4.

Then divide by 2: 4 ÷ 2 = 2.

The Red Sox are therefore 2 games behind the Yankees.

That one was easy because they were 2 games apart in wins and in losses. Sometimes teams will have played different numbers of games at a certain time in the season because of their schedules and because sometimes games are rained out.

To see how many games back the Orioles are behind the Yankees, you would use the same formula.

Wins, 60 – 54 = 6.

Losses, 48 – 40 = 8.

Then add them together: 6 + 8 = 14.

Then divide by 2: 14 ÷ 2 = 7.

The Orioles are 7 games behind the Yankees.

Now, without looking below, try to figure out how far the Blue Jays are behind the Yankees.

Wins, 60 – 49 = 11.

Losses, 50 – 40 = 10.

11 + 10 = 21.

21 ÷ 2 = 10.5

Now you try Tampa Bay! (In case you're wondering, Tampa Bay is 20 games out.)

Secret Signals

Use the decoder to figure out what message the catcher signaled to the pitcher when the crab came up to bat.

A G N S

C H O T

E I P U

F L R Y

All-Time Record Holders

These records are correct as of the start of the 2010 season.

Hitting

All-Time Batting Average Leaders

1. Ty Cobb .366
2. Rogers Hornsby .358
3. "Shoeless" Joe Jackson .356
4. Lefty O'Doul .349
5. Ed Delahanty .346
6. Tris Speaker .345
7. Ted Williams .344
8. Billy Hamilton .344
9. Dan Brouthers .342
10. Babe Ruth .342

A player must have more than 3,000 plate appearances to qualify for this list.

All-Time RBI Leaders

1. Hank Aaron 2,297
2. Babe Ruth 2,213
3. Cap Anson 2,076
4. Barry Bonds 1,996
5. Lou Gehrig 1,995
6. Stan Musial 1,951
7. Ty Cobb 1,938
8. Jimmie Foxx 1,922
9. Eddie Murray 1,917
10. Willie Mays 1,903

Best Live-Ball ERA?

Most of the ERA leaders are from the "Dead-Ball Era," when the ball was softer and harder to hit with any speed. This era lasted until about 1920. So who of the more recent pitchers ranks best in ERA? Mariano Rivera, who comes in seventeenth of all time.

All-Time Home Run Leaders

1. Barry Bonds 762
2. Hank Aaron 755
3. Babe Ruth 714
4. Willie Mays 660
5. Ken Griffey Jr.* 630
6. Sammy Sosa 609
7. Frank Robinson 586
T8. Mark McGwire 583
T8. Alex Rodriguez* 583
10. Harmon Killebrew 573

*Active player as of 2009

Most Hits: Pete Rose at 4,256, followed by Ty Cobb at 4,191. They are the only two players with more than 4,000 hits!

Most Grand Slam Home Runs: Lou Gehrig 23

Most Stolen Bases: Rickey Henderson 1,395

Most At Bats: Pete Rose 14,053

Most Seasons Played: Nolan Ryan 27

Pitching

All-Time Wins Leaders

1. Cy Young 511
2. Walter Johnson 417
T3. Grover Alexander 373
T3. Christy Mathewson 373
5. Pud Gavin 365
6. Warren Spahn 363
7. Kid Nichols 361
8. Greg Maddux 355
9. Roger Clemens 354

All-Time Strikeout Leaders

1. Nolan Ryan 5,174
2. Randy Johnson* 4,875
3. Roger Clemens 4,672
4. Steve Carlton 4,136
5. Bert Blyleven 3,701
6. Tom Seaver 3,640
7. Don Sutton 3,574
8. Gaylord Perry 3,534
9. Walter Johnson 3,508
10. Greg Maddux 3,371

*Active player total at the start of the 2009 season

Lowest All-Time ERA: (2,000 or more innings) Ed Walsh 1.82
Most All-Time Saves: Trevor Hoffman 591, followed by Mariano Rivera at 526 (Saves became an official statistic in 1969.)
Most No-Hitters: Nolan Ryan 7

One Season Records

Hitting

Most Doubles: Earl Webb 67, Boston Red Sox 1931
Most Triples: Chief Wilson 36, Pittsburgh Pirates 1912
Most Home Runs: Barry Bonds 73, San Francisco Giants 2001
Most Runs Batted In: Hack Wilson 191, Chicago Cubs 1930
Most Hits: Ichiro Suzuki 262, Seattle Mariners 2004
Highest Batting Average (500+ Plate Appearances): Hugh Duffy .438, 1894
Highest Average (500+ Plate Appearances) since 1900: Rogers Hornsby .424, St. Louis Cardinals 1924

FUN FACT

Consecutive Scoreless Innings

Dodgers pitcher Orel Hershiser threw 59 straight innings without giving up a run in September of 1988, breaking Dodger Don Drysdale's previous record.

Manager Wins

The manager with the most all-time wins is Connie Mack, who won 3,731 games over 53 years between 1894 and 1950. His record has a lot to do with the many years he was a manager —he actually lost more games than he won! On the other hand, Joe McCarthy managed teams to 2,125 wins, but he only lost 1,333 games for a winning percentage of .615—the best of all time.

How come Drew never finishes a baseball game?

To find out, cross out all the words that have three letters or the letter U!

AND	EVERY	CAT
TIME	GOT	HE
BAT	GETS	FAR
TO	FUR	THIRD
BUT	BASE	HIT
HE	HAT	GOES
HUT	HOME	BAG

Most Stolen Bases: Rickey Henderson 130, Oakland Athletics 1982

Pitching

Most Wins: Jack Chesbro 41, New York Highlanders 1904

Most Strikeouts: Nolan Ryan 383, California Angels 1973; Sandy Koufax 382, Los Angeles Dodgers, 1965

Lowest Earned Run Average: Dutch Leonard 1.01, Boston Red Sox 1914

Most Shutouts: Grover Alexander 16, Philadelphia Phillies 1916

Most Saves: Bobby Thigpen 57, Chicago White Sox 1990

Chapter 8
Keeping Score

Keeping score is a fun way to keep track of what's happening on the field, and it will give you a lasting record of the game you watched. You can buy scorecards at the ballpark or make your own on a sheet of paper. To make life a little easier, you can use the one in this book as a model. The most important thing is that you have a place to write the name of each player and boxes for all nine (or more) innings so that you can put down what they do with each at bat. Names run down the left side of the page and innings run across the top. Why not try scoring the next game you go to?

Scoring Symbols

Scoring is pretty easy once you know the symbols to put in the boxes. You are writing down what the batter does each time he bats. Most of the time you will be listing hits or outs. When the batter makes an out, he either hit the ball to a fielder, or he struck out. For scoring purposes, the fielders are numbered—this number has nothing to do with the numbers the players are wearing on their uniforms; instead, it describes the position played by each player:

Numbers for fielding
1. Pitcher
2. Catcher
3. First baseman
4. Second baseman
5. Third baseman
6. Shortstop
7. Left fielder
8. Center fielder
9. Right fielder

Keeping Score

Let's say the ball is hit in the air to the center fielder and he makes the catch for an out. You would put "8" in the box on your scorecard. If the ball went to right field, you'd put "9," and if it went to left field, you'd put "7." If the player pops it up and it's caught by the first baseman, you'd put "3." If the second baseman catches it, you'd put "4." A line drive to the first baseman could be scored "3L."

If the ball is hit on the ground to the shortstop and he throws to first, you put down both numbers since they were both part of the play. Therefore, a groundout to shortstop would be 6-3. A groundout to second base would be 4-3, a groundout to third base 5-3. If the first baseman picked up a groundball and the pitcher came over to cover first base, caught the throw, and stepped on the base for the out, it would be scored 3-1, because the first baseman is "3" and the pitcher is "1." A double play that goes from the shortstop to the second baseman to the first baseman would be scored DP 6-4-3.

pickoff: If the pitcher throws to a base and gets the runner out before he can get back to the base, it's called a pickoff. To score a pickoff at first base, write PO 1-3, meaning pickoff, pitcher to first baseman.

intentional walk: Sometimes the pitcher walks a batter on purpose; this is called an intentional walk. Sometimes an intentional walk makes it easier to get a double play; other times, the pitcher walks a good hitter so he can pitch to a weaker hitter later in the lineup. Score an intentional walk as "IW" or "IBB."

How to Score Hits

On the sample scorecard on page 139, the way a batter reached base is written outside the diamond. However, some people prefer to write how the batter reached base in the middle of the diamond. Either way works—do whatever makes sense to you.

Whatever fielders are involved in making the out are included in your scoring. Once you memorize the fielders' numbers it becomes very easy.

Hits can be scored in a few ways. A single is either "1B" or a single line (–), a double is "2B" or a double line (=), a triple is 3B or a triple line (≡), and a home run is "HR" or four lines (≣)

When runners get on base you keep track of them using the diamond in the box on the scorecard.

Just draw a line for each base they get to. For example, if a player reaches first base, you would draw the line going from home to first base. If he moves to second base when the next hitter gets a single, you would darken the line going from first base to second base.

As the players move around the bases, you draw the lines of the diamond to follow them. For every run scored you make a complete diamond. If a player is tagged out or stranded on base at the end of the inning, you just leave the diamond incomplete.

There are many, many variations on scoring. Sportswriters, broadcasters, fans, and official team statisticians are all keeping score, and they're all doing it in a slightly different manner from each other. Since there are so many ways to score, there are hundreds of different styles of scorecards. As long as you can follow what is going on in the game and you are having fun, that's all that really matters.

Other Scoring Symbols

More things happen in baseball games than just hits and outs. Here is a more thorough list of the common scoring symbols. To use these, just write the symbol in the box of the player who was out or advanced a base.

WORDS to KNOW

commentators: The commentators are the people who describe the game for the radio or television audience. They must keep detailed scorecards so they can tell the audience what has happened in the game.

BB   Base on balls; or, you can write W for walk

K   Strikeout. If the batter struck out looking (meaning he just stood there while the umpire called a pitch over home plate for strike three) then you can write a backwards K.

HBP   Hit by pitch

SF   Sacrifice fly

S or SAC   Sacrifice bunt

E#   Error, followed by the number of the fielder that made the error. For example, an error by the second baseman would be written E4.

DP   Double play (including the fielder numbers involved in the play)

TP   Triple play (including the fielder numbers involved in the play). Triple plays are extremely rare, so if you score one of these, save the scorecard.

G   Ground ball. If it's not clear that the ball was hit on the ground, write a G.

L   Line drive

F   Usually means that the ball was in foul territory when it was caught. A foul pop up to the catcher would be scored 2F.

The Difference Between Radio and Television

Phil Rizzuto, the Hall of Fame Yankee shortstop of the 1950s, became a commentator with the Yankees after he retired. Rizzuto once said: "I like radio better than television because if you make a mistake on radio, they don't know. You can make up anything on the radio."

Other symbols you might use that don't describe what the batter did, but often tell you that the runners moved up, can be put in a corner of the box:

SB   Stolen base

CS   Caught stealing (include the fielder numbers involved in the play)

PB   Passed ball—this is when the catcher drops a ball he should have caught, allowing a runner to advance

WP   Wild pitch—this is when a pitch is so bad that the catcher didn't have a good chance to catch it, and a runner advances.

This game goes on, and on, and on...

Extra Innings

Use the clue under the blank space to come up with a word. Write this word in the box. When you add the word "IN", the new word has a totally different meaning!

1. _____ IN = to start
(to plead for money)

2. _____ IN = small house in the woods
(taxi)

3. _____ IN = springtime bird with red breast
(steal)

4. _____ IN = heavy, shiny fabric
(past tense of sit)

5. _____ IN = penguin-like bird with colorful beak
(short breath out)

Keeping Score

Baseball Scoring Questions and Answers

Here are some frequently asked questions about scorekeeping.

How Do You Decide Who Is the Winning Pitcher?

Every game has a winning and losing pitcher. The winning pitcher is the one who was pitching for the winning team at the time they took the lead and did not lose the lead again.

For example, if Josh Beckett starts a game for the Red Sox against the Indians and the Red Sox take a 4–0 lead in the early innings and go on to win the game 4–3, Beckett will be the winning pitcher since they never gave up the lead.

However, if the Indians come back and tie the game and the Red Sox bring in a relief pitcher in the seventh inning and then score two runs in the eighth and win 6–4, the relief pitcher would get the win because he was the pitcher when his team took the lead and didn't lose it again.

Starting pitchers get more wins because they pitch more innings. A starting pitcher must go five innings to earn a win, but a reliever can earn the win no matter how few batters he faces.

Losing pitchers are determined in the opposite way. If a pitcher gives up the runs that put the other team ahead and his team never catches up, then he gets the loss.

What Does the Official Scorer Do?

The official scorer is someone at every game whose job is to decide how to score certain plays. When a fielder drops a ball or throws a ball badly, the scorer will decide if it is a

---

FUN FACT

Dropped Third Strikes

When first base is open or when there are two outs, the catcher must hold on to the third strike. If he drops the ball, he must get the out by tagging the batter or throwing to first base. Usually, the catcher does this without trouble. However, if the third strike was a wild pitch, or if the catcher makes a bad throw to first, the runner could be safe; but the pitcher still gets statistical credit for a strikeout. If this happens, on your scorecard you would write K-E2 (if the catcher made a bad throw) or K-WP (if the pitcher made a wild pitch).

The First Scorecard

The first scorecard was created by the Knickerbocker ball club way back in 1845.

hit or an error. Official scorers also decide whether a pitch is a wild pitch or a passed ball, and they make other, more obscure scoring decisions. Official scorers decide only how the game is recorded statistically—they cannot overrule an umpire's call.

Why Do the Managers and Umpires Meet at Home Plate Before Every Game?

You may notice that before each game there is a short meeting between the umpires and the managers or coaches. This meeting has two purposes. The first is to exchange the lineup cards—each manager hands the umpire and the opposing manager a copy of his lineup. After the meeting, no more changes are allowed to the lineup.

The second purpose is to discuss the ground rules. Every stadium is built differently, and it's important that everyone understands the specific rules for what is considered in-play and what is foul territory. Some ballparks have a line on a high fence. If the ball is over that line it's a home run. Other stadiums have a high wall, but the rule is if it hits the wall, it's not a home run but still in play. Everything about the field needs to be talked about so there are no problems with the rules during the game. You probably do the same thing before playing any game with your friends, when you stop and go over the rules.

A Portion of a Sample Scorecard

You learned how to read the box score from the October 2, 2004, game between the Dodgers and the Giants. On page 139 is the Dodgers' half of a scorecard from that game.

The Magic Number

Near the end of the baseball season teams start to figure out the "magic number." This is how many games the leading team must win, and how many games any other team must lose, for the leader to win the pennant (championship in their league).

There's some tricky math here. Pretend you have two teams—Team A and Team X. Team A is the leading team in the league, having won the most games so far. Team X is any other team in the league.

Follow the steps below using the scores from our sample teams. You can use the same steps with your favorite teams!

The season has 162 scheduled games.

	won	lost	games played so far:
TEAM A	93	59	152
TEAM X	89	63	

Games TEAM X has won _____

ADD games TEAM X has left _____

SUBTRACT games TEAM A has won _____

ADD the number 1 _____

THE MAGIC NUMBER

Most of this game was pretty easy to score. For example, look at the fourth inning: Finley flied out to right field, Beltre flied out to center field, and Green flied out to center field. In fact, one of the things this scorecard can tell you that the box score can't is that the Dodgers hit a lot of fly balls, but that most of them were caught.

When a pinch hitter comes to the plate, you draw a heavy line before the box when he comes up. Look at Mayne's spot in the seventh inning. The heavy line means that Mayne was replaced with pinch hitter Grabowski; but the K means that Grabowski struck out.

When a new pitcher comes into the game, you draw a heavy line before the first batter he faces. For example, in the eighth inning, a new pitcher came in to face Finley, and another new pitcher came in to face Beltre.

The ninth inning of this scorecard is kind of complicated. Go through it batter by batter to find out what happened. Green led off the inning with a single, and then Ventura walked. Cora struck out looking. Hernandez pinch-hit, and he walked to load the bases. Choi pinch-hit, and he also walked, forcing in a run. A new pitcher came in. Izturis reached first base on an error by the shortstop, scoring Ventura. A new pitcher came in. Werth singled, scoring a third run. Another new pitcher came in. (That's a lot of pitchers for one inning.) Then Finley hit a home run to win the game—the GS stands for grand slam. Since this inning had so much going on and was so exciting, you might choose to make a few notes about it at the bottom of the scorecard page. Now, if you're a Dodgers fan, you might ask Steve Finley to autograph this scorecard, frame it, and put it on the wall of your room. Of course, if you're a Giants fan, you might just put the scorecard in your desk drawer and try to forget about it.

Sample Scorecard

This is how a finished scorecard might look.

DATE: October 2, 2004
Los Angeles Dodgers (vs. San Francisco Giants) at Dodger Stadium

FINAL SCORE: SF 3 LA 7

Pos.	Name	1	2	3	4	5	6	7	8	9	10	11
SS	Izturis	G3		8		2F			8	◆ E6	RBI	
LF	Werth	K		8			3		1B	◆ 1B	RBI	
CF	Finley	1B			9		4L		4-3 / HR	◆	^{4}RBI	
3B	Beltre	8			8		5-3		6-3 / GS			
RF	Green		1B		8			9		◆ 1B		
1B	Ventura		K			3-1		K		◆ W		
2B	Cora		5			E8 / W		W		K		
C	Mayne/ PH Grabowski (7th), PH J. Hernandez (9th)		9					K		◆ W		
P	Dessens/ PH Saenz (8th), PH Choi (9th)			7		5-3			1B	◆ W	RBI	

What kind of baseball players practice in the Arctic Circle?

Color in each box with a dot in the upper right-hand corner to find the silly answer to this riddle:

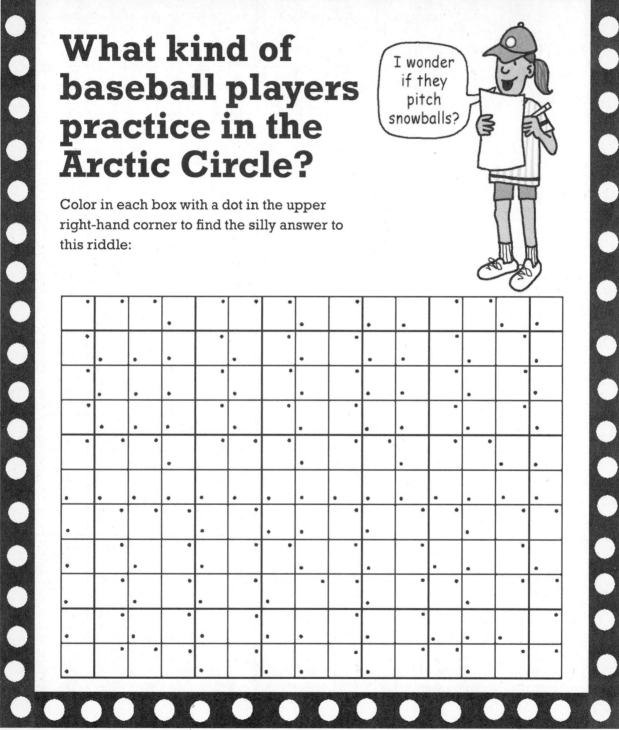

Baseball fans love to go to games, watch games on TV, read about games, and tell stories about games. But there are even more ways to enjoy baseball! This chapter describes three popular baseball-related activities: collecting baseball cards, playing fantasy baseball, and playing a card game that was inspired by baseball. Even if you've never tried these activities before, you might find that they are great ways to gain more knowledge of baseball, meet and hang out with fellow fans, and enjoy a new hobby.

Baseball Cards

Baseball cards are the size of playing cards. They have a picture of a player on one side; the other side lists his career stats and a short description of his career highlights. Your card collection is a reflection of your favorite teams and your favorite players, but as you get older your collection can help you remember past seasons.

Acquiring Baseball Cards

You can buy baseball cards in lots of different places. Grocery or convenience stores will often have packs of cards. Department stores or discount outlets might have a wider selection. Specialist card stores and dealers will have rare or especially interesting cards.

Cards come in packs of seven, ten, twelve, or more, depending on the company and the type of pack you buy. Many companies make baseball cards, each with a different look. Topps, Donruss, and Upper Deck are among the most popular card-making companies. Most packs include a random assortment of current players—the fun is seeing which players you get when you open the pack. New cards come out every season, as they have since the early 1900s.

Most card buyers enjoy collecting the cards for the fun of it. The cards themselves have a glossy look and the photos are sometimes really cool action shots from the game. The statistics on the back of the cards give you all sorts of information about how the player has done in his career. Reading your cards can teach you a lot about your favorite players, so the next time you see them in a game, you have a better appreciation for who they are and where they've come from.

There are more serious collectors who buy and sell older or special cards for lots of money. Card shows, online card dealers, and auctions are places where adults who are in the baseball card business can buy and sell valuable cards. But baseball card collecting is not about monetary value—it's about savoring the game of baseball.

WORDS to KNOW

commons: Commons are cards of average players, not superstars. These cards aren't usually valuable to professional collectors, but they might still have value to you if the player is one of your favorites or if he plays for your favorite team.

Dugout

One letter has been dug out of each of the following common baseball words. Fill in the missing letters. Then, transfer those letters to the corresponding boxes in the grid to form the answer to this riddle:

What's another nickname for a baseball bat?

1. UNI _ ORM
2. G _ OVE
3. PLA _ OFF
4. _ LIDE
5. S _ ING
6. F _ N
7. BUN _
8. CA _ CHER
9. ST _ AL
10. _ UN

1	2	3	4	5	6	7	8	9	10

Collectible Cards

Sometimes the most valuable cards are those that accidentally get printed with a few mistakes or differences. Can you find the nine differences between these two cards?

Collectible Words

See if you can collect nine words hiding in the word **COLLECTIBLE**.

Extra Fun: Try to have all nine words use only four letters.

Some Baseball Card History

Professional baseball began at the end of the 1860s, and the first baseball cards were printed by the late 1880s. These early cards were printed on the cardboard backs of cigarette packs. Top players of the day like Cap Anson and Buck Ewing were among the first players to appear on cards. Pretty soon, in the early 1900s, a number of cigarette manufacturers were printing cards of the best players, such as Ty Cobb and Honus Wagner. There were far fewer copies of each card printed than there are of cards today.

By the 1930s chewing gum companies were also making baseball cards, and collecting these cards was becoming more popular. In 1933 the Goudey Chewing Gum Company accidentally forgot to print card number 106 in their set, a card of all-star (and future Hall-of-Famer) Napoleon LaJoie. So many collectors sent letters asking for the missing card that the company had to print more in 1934, and it sent them to the people who had written in. This was one of the first indications that card collecting was becoming popular.

Then, in 1952, Topps made its first baseball cards with statistics of the players on the back. Card collecting was very popular through the 1960s and 1970s, but it wasn't until the late 1980s that rich collectors began to pay high prices for old cards. Some people began to see baseball cards as an investment, like putting money in the stock market. Today, card collecting isn't quite as popular as it was at the start of the 1990s, but many, many fans still savor their collections.

Why Do Some Cards Cost More Than Others?

For one thing, the greater players are more expensive because everyone knows them. Older cards, like those from the 1940s, 1950s, or 1960s usually cost more than cards

---

Stick of Gum

Once upon a time, one of the things you would always find in a pack of baseball cards was a long, pink stick of chewing gum. This isn't very common anymore, but it was standard for many years.

The Most Expensive Card Ever

Pirates shortstop Honus Wagner did not want his card associated with cigarettes, so he asked that the tobacco company stop printing his cards. Therefore, only a few cards of this legendary player exist. His 1909 card, known to collectors as T-206, is now so rare that at an auction in New York City it sold for $640,000.

from the 1970s or 1980s because they are harder to find. Not many people saved them, so they are more expensive since there aren't too many around. When a lot of people want something, like a rare card, the person who owns it can ask for more money since people can't go out and find that card elsewhere. Cards that have a "defect," or a mistake, on them are also expensive since they are very rare; usually, the company corrected the mistake after they printed the first few. Sometimes a word is off-center or even spelled wrong. A couple of times a company printed the wrong name with the wrong picture. Now that's a big mistake—and an expensive card!

Sometimes the cost might depend on where you are buying a card. For example, an Albert Pujols rookie card would sell for more in St. Louis than in New York because he is a Cardinals fan favorite. But a Derek Jeter card would be more expensive in New York than in St. Louis because he is a Yankee.

What Should You Do with Your Baseball Cards?

The easy answer to that question is—anything you want, especially anything that makes collecting cards fun. Here are some ideas of ways to enjoy your collection.

- **Read your cards.** You may think you know everything about your favorite player, but you might be surprised by some new information on that player's card. You might learn something about a player that makes you like him more—for example, he may have grown up in your hometown, or he may have gone to your favorite college.
- **Trade with your friends.** If you are buying lots of packs of cards, you will end up with several copies

of the same player's card. Offer to give a duplicate to a friend if your friend will give you a card that you really want. Or, say you're trying to collect the whole starting lineup for your favorite team. You might be able to fill in the cards you don't have by trading.

- **Use cards as decorations.** Is the wall behind your desk or over your bed bare? Does your locker need something on the door? Use baseball cards to decorate. You could change the players you have on display every month or every year based on how the players do.

- **Collect groups of players that are special.** Of course, you want to collect cards of your favorite players. But you might also try to get the whole roster of your town's home team. Or this year's all-star team. Or the ten pitchers with the most victories. Or the batters who lead the league in home runs, RBIs, and batting average. Or last year's MVPs and Cy Young Award winners. Pick any category of players that interests you, and go get their cards!

- **Make albums.** You can organize your cards in photo albums, or even in albums specially designed for baseball cards. Albums allow you to look at many sets of cards at once; they also keep the cards in good condition in a place where you won't lose them.

- **Get autographs.** If you know that you might have a chance to get a player's autograph—say, you have front-row tickets to a game, or you're going to hear a player speak—bring that player's card and ask him to sign it.

- **Anything else you can think of!** Some people think of their cards as a financial investment. They collect cards only because they think the cards will be worth lots of money someday. Well, it's extremely unlikely

that your card collection will ever be worth much more than you paid for it. So if you want to put baseball cards in the spokes of your bicycle, play games with them outside, or tack them to your wall, do it! The whole point of card collecting is to have fun. Anything you can do with your cards that you think is fun is worth doing.

Fantasy Baseball

Have you ever wanted to own a baseball team? If so, you should start saving your money now—it costs close to $1 billion to buy a major-league team. But you and your friends can run your own fantasy baseball teams this season without paying any money at all.

In fantasy baseball, you choose major-league players to be on your team. The better your players perform, the better your team does. Since you're in charge of your team, you can make trades, bench players who aren't doing well, set starting lineups, put players on the disabled list—pretty much everything a real baseball owner does.

How Fantasy Baseball Works

Fantasy baseball teams are ranked based on statistics. Usually a league keeps track of ten categories. Your team gets credit for the statistics of all players in your starting lineup. If one of your players hits a home run, your team gets a home run. If one of your pitchers strikes out eight batters, your team adds eight strikeouts to its total.

In head-to-head fantasy leagues, you play a "game" against another team in your league each week. You have to do better than your opponent in each category. For example, if your pitchers record five saves this week and your

Which Stats Does Your League Use?

Leagues usually keep track of ten statistics. For offensive players, your team earns points for batting average, home runs, runs batted in, stolen bases, and runs. Pitchers earn points for wins, saves, strikeouts, earned run average, and base runners per inning. But you can find (or create) a league that keeps track of pretty much any stats.

opponent's pitchers only record four saves, then you win the "saves" category. If you win more categories than your opponent, then you win the game! Whichever team wins the most games by the end of the year is the champion.

In rotisserie leagues, you add up your statistics for the whole season. You get points for every team you beat in each category. Whoever gets the most points at the end of the season is the league champion.

Determining Who's on Your Team

All fantasy baseball owners want Albert Pujols on their team. But he can only be on one team in each league. So how do you decide who gets which players? There are two common methods: the draft and the auction. The draft is simpler and is the best way to go if you're new to fantasy baseball. Advanced players can try out an auction.

In a fantasy baseball draft, teams take turns selecting players. On your turn, you can choose any player who hasn't already been chosen. But you have to be sure to fill every position on your team!

In an auction, each team is given a budget of pretend money, say, $100. A player is mentioned, then each team can bid for that player. Whoever bids the most money gets the player. But you only have that $100 for your whole team. If you spend too much on one player, you'll be stuck without money to fill out your roster.

After the draft or auction, you still have to manage your team. If one of your players gets hurt or isn't doing well, you'll need to replace him. The easiest way to obtain players is through "waivers." Players who aren't on a team are listed on the "waiver wire." You can choose a player from this list to be on your team. Each league makes rules about how

WHIP: WHIP stands for "Walks plus Hits per Inning Pitched." Many leagues keep track of this category, which means almost the same thing as base runners per inning. Only the very best pitchers' WHIPs are below 1.000. A good WHIP is 1.100 or 1.150.

Keepers: Once you've played fantasy baseball with the same people for a few years, you might make a rule that owners can choose some players from this year's team to be on their team again next year. A player who stays with the same team two years in a row is called a "keeper."

often you can pick up one of these players, and about what happens if two teams want the same player.

Another option for improving your team is to make trades. If your team has plenty of one statistic but needs to do better in another, you might consider a trade. For example, your team might have a whole lot of saves, but not very many stolen bases. So, you could offer to give another team one of your closers, like Mariano Rivera, in exchange for someone who steals a lot of bases, like Jose Reyes.

Fantasy Baseball Strategy

The fantasy team owners who do the best are the ones who pay careful attention to the players. Sure, you want to pick star players, the guys everyone knows about. But pretty soon after your draft starts, there won't be any stars left. So how do you know which players to pick?

Before your draft, you should read about every team. Find out what new players are on the team. Know who is likely to start at each position. Then, make a list of who you think are the best ten or fifteen major league players at each position, and a list of the thirty or so players you absolutely want if you can have them.

After the draft, it's usually a good idea to leave your team alone for a few weeks to see how your players do. Be careful—in the excitement of the early season, it's tempting to give up on a good player who starts with a slump; you might want to pick up a poorer player who happens to be off to a hot start. More often than not, though, you'll do best by sticking with your players who have a history of producing strong stats. But if one of your players is injured, or if he starts losing playing time—then it might be time to make a move.

Who Keeps Track of Your League?

Years ago, people who played fantasy baseball had to keep careful track of their team by reading newspaper box scores every day and writing down each player's stats. Nowadays, though, the Internet makes keeping track of your team's stats simple. Some Internet fantasy baseball services are free, like those at *www.yahoo.com* or *www.cbssports.com*. For your first season of fantasy baseball, a free service will work fine—your parents can easily help you sign up with one of these.

Other websites require a registration fee to play. These sites will usually provide more options in terms of the stats your league can use, and you'll usually get more detailed (maybe even live) scoring updates, message boards, and "expert" advice. But you don't need to pay to play fantasy baseball unless you're an advanced enough player to really want these extra features.

The neatest thing about fantasy baseball is how much you learn about major league players. Fantasy leagues also give you baseball topics to talk to your friends about. Try owning a team for a season—your fantasy experience will probably allow you to appreciate the real game of baseball even more.

Playing Card Baseball

This game was invented years ago, long before computers and video games. You don't need much equipment—just some playing cards and perhaps paper and pencil. It helps to know how to keep score to a game (see Chapter 8), but you can play even if you don't know how to keep score. This can be fun to play with a friend, but you can also play both teams by yourself.

Flash in the Pan

In 2006, Chris Shelton of the Tigers hit nine home runs in just the first two weeks of the season! Some fantasy owners rushed to pick him up . . . but he hit only seven more homers all year. Oops.

cheat sheets: Rankings of the best players are called "cheat sheets." Don't start a draft without one! You can make cheat sheets yourself or you can use one from a magazine or website.

First, write down two lineups of nine players each. Shuffle the deck and turn over three cards. The third card is what the batter does. You turn over three per hitter until there are three outs. Then you reshuffle the entire deck for the other team and turn over three cards at a time until that team gets three outs. Score as you would a regular baseball game, or in any way you can make up.

What the Cards Mean

- 2, 3, 4, 5, 6, 7, 8, and red 9s are outs
- Black 9s are walks
- 10s are strikeouts
- Jacks are singles; red jacks move base runners two bases, black jacks move runners one base
- Queens are doubles; red queens let base runners on second score, black queens mean runners advance only one base
- Red kings are triples; black kings are like black jacks— they are singles (because there aren't too many triples hit in baseball)
- Aces are home runs

You can make one card in the deck an error card, meaning the batter reached base on an error. For a high-scoring game use all fifty-two cards, or even two decks. For a game with lower scoring, take out some aces and one of the red kings. You can add your own features to the game, such as a certain card for base stealing or allowing the better hitters to get hits on red 9s. Make up new rules as you go and see how they work!

Name Game

This baseball card collector has gotten some pretty famous autographs. Unfortunately, the players signed their names too big! Can you tell who signed each card? Choose names from the list.

Barry Bonds
Willie Mays
Nolan Ryan
Pete Rose
Alex Rodrigue:
Cy Young
Sandy Koufax
Ty Cobb
Jimmie Foxx
Tom Seaver
Greg Maddux
Lou Gehrig
Hank Aaron

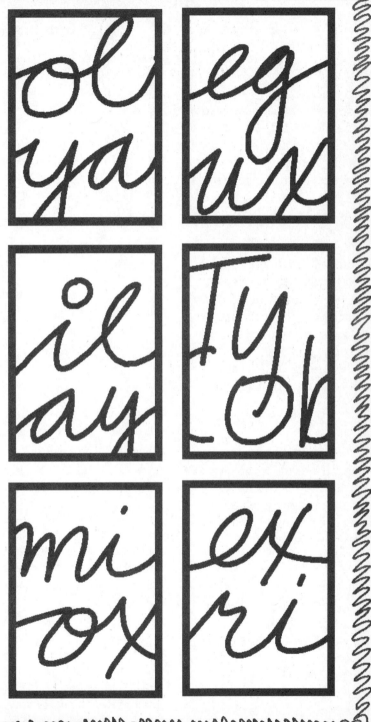

assist

When a player makes a throw of any kind to get an out, whether it's an infielder throwing a batter out running to first base or an outfielder throwing a runner out at home plate, the player gets an assist.

backstop

The fence behind home plate is the backstop. In parks and on little league fields, the backstop is usually a high fence that slants over home plate so that foul balls don't fly off and hurt people passing by. (Backstop is also a slang term used for a catcher.)

battery

Battery is a term for the pitcher and catcher. If, for example, Joe Nathan is pitching and Joe Mauer is catching, they are "the battery" in that game.

batting order

The order in which players on a team come up and take their turn as the hitter. The manager or coach of the team decides the batting order before the game and lists the players, first through ninth, in order of when

they will hit. If a batter bats out of turn he can be called out.

bleachers

The seats behind the outfield wall are called the bleachers. Sometimes, like in Wrigley Field, the fans who sit there call themselves the "bleacher bums."

blooper

A blooper is a ball that is not hit very hard but sort of pops over the infielders and lands in front of the outfielders for a hit.

box score

A box score is a grid containing a summary of the game statistics, including how each player did.

bullpen

The bullpen is where the relief pitchers warm up before coming in to pitch. Most stadiums have bullpens beyond the outfield fences, while some have them in foul territory.

bunt

To bunt is to hold the bat horizontally, one hand on the handle and the other way up on the bat (don't hold it with

your hand around the front of the bat, just pinch it from the back part so your finger doesn't get squished by the pitch). The idea is to let the ball just bounce off the bat and stay fair so the runners can move up a base, which is known as a "sacrifice." You can also bunt for a hit by pushing the bat so that the ball rolls a little farther toward third base or first base.

cleanup hitter

The cleanup hitter is the fourth hitter in the lineup.

closer

The relief pitcher that comes in to get the final outs and the save is the team's "closer."

commentators

The commentators are the broadcasters or announcers who are at the ballpark describing what is going on in the game on either television or radio.

commons

Commons are cards of average players, not superstars. These cards aren't usually valuable to professional collectors; but they still might have value to you or

to a friend if the player is one of your favorites, or if that player is on your favorite team.

contact hitter

A contact hitter is one that makes contact with the ball often and doesn't strike out very much.

count

The count is the number of balls and strikes that have been pitched to the hitter. For example, two balls and two strikes would be a "two and two" count.

dinger

Dinger is a slang term for a home run.

disabled list

When a player is injured the team may put the player on what is called "the disabled list," or DL. This means the player cannot play for fifteen or more days and the team can call someone else up from the minor leagues to put on their roster of active players.

double

A hit that gets the batter safely to second base.

double play

A double play is when two players get called out after one player hits the ball.

error

When a fielder drops or bobbles a ball or throws it so the other fielder can't catch it and it results in the batter or runner being safe, it's called an error on the fielder.

extra innings

If a game is tied after the regulation nine innings, teams go into extra innings, which means they play additional innings until someone scores the winning run or runs. The home team always gets the last turn at bat.

fan

Besides being one of the people rooting for your favorite team, to "fan" in baseball is another term for striking out.

foul ball

A ball that is hit that is not in fair territory. Foul balls count as strike one and strike two, but not as strike three unless you're bunting. In the big leagues, many foul balls go into the stands and are souvenirs to the fans who catch them.

foul line

The lines extending from home plate past first and third base all the way to the outfield fence that separate fair territory from foul territory. A fly ball that lands on the foul line is fair.

foul out

When a ball is hit in the air in foul territory and caught by an opposing player for an out.

foul pole

A ball that flies over the outfield fence is only a home run if it leaves the field in fair territory. The foul poles make it easy to tell whether a ball is a home run: One side of the pole is fair, the other is foul. But if the ball hits the foul pole, it's a home run.

foul territory

The part of the playing field that is outside of the foul lines and not part of the actual field of play.

full count

Three balls and two strikes is considered a full count—one more ball is a walk and one more strike is a strikeout.

grand slam

A grand slam is when you hit a home run with the bases loaded (a player on each base). The most runs you can score on one hit are on a grand slam!

head-to-head

A type of fantasy league in which your team's stats are compared to one other team's stats on a week-by-week basis.

hit and run

A "hit and run" play is where the base runners start running and the batter is supposed to hit the ball on the ground or for a base hit. This play helps avoid a double play and can also get runners to advance more bases on a base hit.

hits

A player gets a hit when he or she hits the ball and then runs to the base without making an out. Here are the different kinds of hits you can get: single, double, triple, and home run.

home run

You touch all the bases including home plate (where you start from as the batter). If you hit one over the fence, it's a home run and you should be very happy!

home team

The team most of the local fans root for since they are the team hosting the game on their field. The home team always bats second in the inning, or in the "bottom of the inning."

inning

An inning is a period of play in which each team has a turn at bat. Each team gets three outs. A regulation major-league game lasts nine innings.

inside-the-park home run

Most home runs go over the outfield fence, but a fast runner might be able to get all the way around the bases on a ball that stays in the ballpark on an inside-the-park homer—it's very rare!

intentional walk

An intentional walk is when a pitcher walks a batter on purpose. Sometimes this makes it easier to get a double play if there are other runners on second and/or third. Sometimes a batter is walked intentionally because the player is very good and the pitcher doesn't want to give up a home run.

left on base

You may see this in the box score (lob) or hear broadcasters mention it. This indicates how many players were left standing on the bases when the final out was made to end an inning.

mound

The mound, or pitching mound, is the dirt circle in the middle of the infield diamond where the pitcher stands. It's called a mound because the pitcher stands almost a foot higher than the rest of the infield.

on deck

The batter who is scheduled to hit next is considered to be waiting "on deck." Usually there is an on-deck circle where the player stands and takes practice swings.

opposite field

When the announcer says a hitter got a hit to the opposite field, it means the ball went the opposite way from where it should go for that type of hitter. When the bat is swung around, most left-handed hitters will hit the ball to right field, and right-handed hitters will hit the ball to left field. If the hitter hits it to the other field, a right-handed hitter hitting to right field and vice versa, it's called hitting to the opposite field.

overrun

This is when you are going too fast and run over the base. You're allowed to overrun first base, but if you overrun second or third, you can be tagged out.

pennant

The team that wins the National League or American League Championship is said to have won the pennant—then they play in the World Series.

pickoff

If there's a base runner and the pitcher throws to the fielder, who catches the runner off base and tags that runner for an out, it's called a pickoff.

pinch hitter

A pinch hitter is a hitter who bats in place of someone else.

pinch runner

A pinch runner is a player who comes in to run for someone else. This may be a faster runner who can steal a base or score a run more easily.

prospect

A player who is thought to have skills that will make that player a future star is considered to be a prospect.

putout

Whenever a fielder catches a ball that results in an out, it's a putout. This includes a first baseman taking a throw from an infielder and stepping on the base, or a catcher on a strikeout.

rain delay

A rain delay is when the game is stopped because of rain, but they hope to continue and finish it later. The umpires decide when to stop, restart, or call a game (cancel it) because of rain.

rain out

A rain out is when a game is called off because of rain. If this happens before the fifth inning, the game doesn't count. If it's after the fifth inning it's considered an official game, and whichever team was ahead at the time wins.

reliever

A reliever or relief pitcher is the pitcher who comes in to replace the starting pitcher.

rookie

A first-year player is also known as a rookie.

roster

A roster is the listing of players on the team. Major-league rosters include twenty-five players for most of the season.

rotisserie

A type of fantasy baseball league in which your team's stats are compared to other team's stats for the whole year.

run

A "run" in baseball is scored whenever a player comes all the way around the bases and crosses home plate. The team who scores the most runs wins.

rundown play

When a runner is trapped between bases, the fielders play what looks like a game of monkey-in-the-middle as they throw the ball back and forth trying to tag the runner and not let him or her get to the next base. Usually a runner will be called out in a rundown play unless one of the fielders misses the ball.

single

You get to first base safely without anyone catching the ball in the air, tagging you out, or throwing to first base before you get there.

save

When a pitcher comes into a close ballgame and gets the final outs it is called a save.

scoring position

When a runner is on second or third base, he is considered in scoring position, meaning it's easier to score on a hit.

signs

Some people hold up signs in the stands, but in baseball there are other signs. The catcher puts down fingers to give the pitcher a sign as to what pitch to throw. There are also signs relayed from the coach at third base to the batter. Coaches are usually busy touching their cap, tugging on their ear, and doing all sorts of movements. They are signaling the batter to take a pitch, swing away, bunt, or perhaps hit and run. They are also often signaling runners on base. Next time you're at a game, watch the third base coach for a minute and see what he's up to. If you're playing, always check what the sign from the coach is before the pitcher pitches.

slide

A slide is when a runner dives feet first or head first into a base. Be careful if you try sliding—ask your coach to help you learn how to slide properly so you don't get hurt.

southpaw

A left-handed pitcher is sometimes referred to as a southpaw.

spitball or "spitter"

Once upon a time, in the early years of baseball, it used to be okay for pitchers to spit on the ball before throwing it. It made the ball make some strange movements, and batters had a hard time hitting it. The rules no longer allow this pitch to be thrown.

starter

The starter is the pitcher that begins pitching the game for the team.

take

To "take" a pitch means to not swing at it. If a pitcher is having trouble throwing strikes, a batter may take a pitch to see if the pitcher can throw it in the strike zone. If the batter has three balls and no strikes, it's a good idea to take the pitch to try and get a walk.

tarp

The tarp is what the grounds crew covers the field with while the teams, umpires, and fans wait for the rain to stop so they can continue the game. The tarp is a giant piece of plastic that usually covers just the infield.

triple

A hit that gets the batter safely to third base.

triple play

A triple play is a very rare play where one player hits the ball and all three outs are made. Naturally, there has to be no one out and at least two runners on base for a triple play.

umpire

An umpire is the person who is refereeing the game or ruling on the plays in the game. The umpire rules whether a pitch is a strike or a ball, if a ball that is hit is fair or foul, or if a batter or runner is safe or out.

visiting team

The team that comes to play on another team's field. The visiting team always bats first in the inning, known as the "top of the inning."

walk-off home run

This refers to a home run in the bottom of the ninth or in the home team's at bat in the bottom of an extra inning that wins and ends the game. Following the home run, the teams walk off the field—hence the name.

WHIP

Walks plus Hits per Inning Pitched is an important statistical category for fantasy baseball. Anything below 1.2 is pretty good.

wild card

In major-league baseball there are three divisions in each league, but four teams make the playoffs each year. The fourth team, the wild card team, is the best second-place team from any one of the three divisions.

Appendix B
Books, Magazines, Websites, and More

Baseball Books

Historical Baseball Books

The Sporting News Selects: Baseball's 25 Greatest Moments by Ron Smith and Joe Morgan

The All-Century Team by Mark Vancil looks at the 100 best players of the 20th century.

The Story of The Negro Leagues by William Brashler has the history and the stars of these leagues.

300 Great Baseball Cards of the 20th Century is a historical look at baseball cards from Beckett Publishing.

The Echoing Green: The Untold Story of Bobby Thomson, Ralph Branca, and the Shot Heard Round the World by Joshua Prager gives details about how the Giants stole catchers' signs from their center field clubhouse, leading to Thomson's famous home run.

How to Play the Game

Jeff Burroughs' Little League Instructional Guide

Baseball for Kids: Skills, Strategies and Stories to Make You a Better Ballplayer by Jerry Kasoff

Touching All the Bases: Baseball for Kids of All Ages by Claire MacKay

The Art of Pitching by Tom Seaver

The Art of Hitting by Tony Gwynn

The Science of Hitting by Ted Williams

Biographies

Jackie and Me (about Jackie Robinson), *Babe and Me*, and *Honus and Me* (about Honus Wagner) by Dan Gutman, from his Baseball Card Adventure series

Lou Gehrig, Pride of the Yankees by Keith Brandt

Babe Ruth, Home Run Hero by Keith Brandt

I Had a Hammer: The Hank Aaron Story by Lonnie Wheeler with Hank Aaron himself

Lists, Quotes, Jokes, and Statistics

Yogisms: I Didn't Really Say Everything I Said by Yogi Berra has a lot of the funniest sayings by one funny former catcher.

Total Baseball: The Official Encyclopedia of Major League Baseball by John Thorn is loaded with statistics and very heavy.

Baseball Prospectus: The Essential Guide to the Baseball Season is a yearly guide that includes comprehensive statistics and analysis. It's a great tool to help prepare for a fantasy baseball season.

Batter Up! Baseball Activities for Kids of All Ages by Ouisie Shapiro includes a lot of fun facts, quizzes, and games. If you like the puzzles in the book you're reading now, check out *Batter Up!*

Baseball Math: Grandslam Activities and Projects for Grades 4–8 by Christopher Jennison will help you work on your math skills while having some fun.

Books, Magazines, Websites, and More

Baseball Movies

The Pride of the Yankees, 1942, the story of Lou Gehrig

The Babe Ruth Story, 1948

The Jackie Robinson Story, 1950

Angels in the Outfield, 1951, the original

Damn Yankees, 1958, a broadway musical brought to film

The Bad News Bears, 1976

The Natural, 1984

Eight Men Out, 1988, about the 1919 Black Sox scandal

Field of Dreams, 1989

Major League, 1989

A League of Their Own, 1992, about the women's leagues of the 1940s

Angels in the Outfield, 1994, the remake

Magazines

Baseball Digest

This is a monthly magazine with stories about pro players past and present, rosters, a quiz (it's not easy), a crossword puzzle, and plenty of fun facts about the game.
www.baseballdigest.com

Baseball Weekly

Baseball Weekly is a magazine devoted to the latest info on the major leagues and even the minor leagues. Plenty of statistics and recent box scores are included in *Baseball Weekly*.

Junior Baseball

Junior Baseball is all about baseball leagues for players 7 to 17.
www.juniorbaseball.com

Sporting News

Sporting News is the weekly newspaper of all sports. During the spring and summer months, there are plenty of stories about baseball plus lots of neat stats.
www.sportingnews.com

Sports Illustrated for Kids

Sports Illustrated for Kids has info on many sports, including baseball. The magazine includes tips on playing the game and interviews with your favorite players.
www.sikids.com

USA Today

USA Today has a great sports section with a lot about baseball, including daily reports on each team so you can see what your favorite team is up to.
www.usatoday.com

Websites

MLB.com

This is the major leagues' official baseball website. You can find anything you need there,
including up-to-the-inning scores, pitching
match-ups for the next several days, injury
reports, trades, news, player statistics, and info
on everything from spring training through the
World Series. There is a history section with
links to all sorts of baseball records and much,
much more. In May and June you can even vote
for the players for the All-Star game.
www.mlb.com

Negro Leagues Baseball

This is a very informative site about the Negro
Leagues. The history, players, and teams are all
part of this interesting site. New books are featured, as are several articles that offer insight
into an important part of baseball and American
history.
www.negroleaguebaseball.com

Appendix C
Puzzle Answers

page 9 • Why do hitters...

Because there are more

to choose from!

page 18 • Stealing Bases

BALTIMORE ORIOLES
BOSTON RED SOX
NEW YORK METS
BROOKLYN DODGERS
LOS ANGELES ANGELS
ATLANTA BRAVES

page 11 • Curve Ball

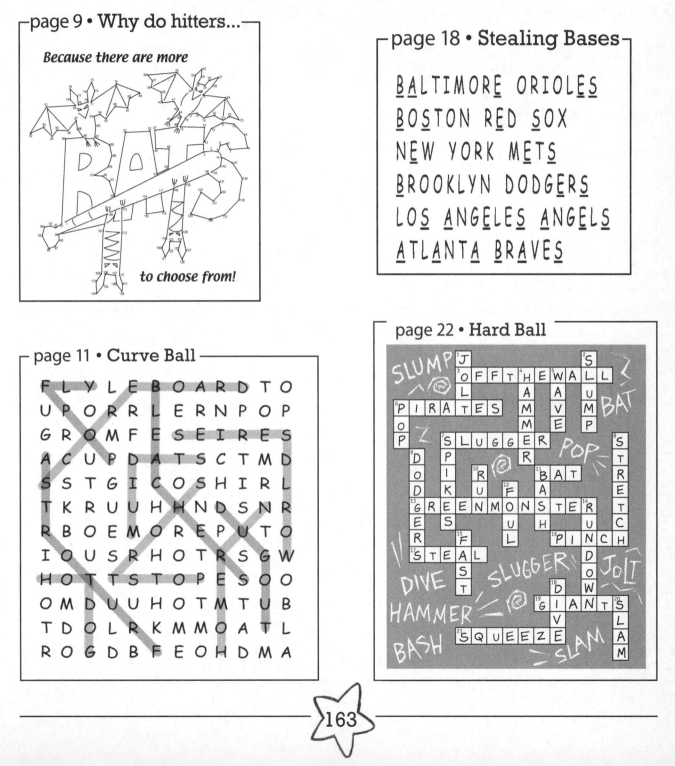

page 22 • Hard Ball

page 34 • Say What?

Y O G I	,	I		C A M E
H E R E		T O		H I T
N O T		T O		R E A D !

YOGI, I CAME HERE TO HIT, NOT TO READ!

page 50 • Play Ball

1. Print the word BASEBALL.	BASEBALL
2. Switch the position of the first two letters.	ABSEBALL
3. Move the 5th letter between the 2nd and 3rd letters.	ABBSEBALL
4. Switch the positions of the 4th and 8th letters.	ABBLEALS
5. Change the 6th letter to P.	ABBLEPLS
6. Change the last letter to E.	ABBLEPLE
7. Change both B's to P's.	APPLEPLE
8. Change the 7th letter to I.	APPLEPIE

page 57 • Switch Hitter

page 61 • Famous Fungo!

_2_ A milk pitcher!

_3_ A catcher's mutt!

_1_ A pancake batter!

page 58 • Who's Who?

1. The Big Train	_3_ Cy Young
2. Tom Terrific	_5_ Jimmy Foxx
3. Cyclone	_4_ Joe DiMaggio
4. Joltin' Joe	_7_ Mickey Mantle
5. Double X	_11_ Ozzie Smith
6. Mr. October	_10_ Pete Rose
7. The Mick	_12_ Randy Johnson
8. Say Hey Kid	_6_ Reggie Jackson
9. Stan The Man	_13_ Roger Clemens
10. Charlie Hustle	_9_ Stan Musial
11. Wizard of Oz	_2_ Tom Seaver
12. The Big Unit	_1_ Walter Johnson
13. The Rocket	_8_ Willie Mays

page 71 • Hink Pinks

1. The heavier of two batters.

FATTER BATTER

2. Where you throw a bad referee.

UMP DUMP

3. Nine baseball players shouting at once.

TEAM SCREAM

4. The last part of a baseball game when one team has more points.

WINNING INNING

Puzzle Answers

page 72 • Baseball Diamond

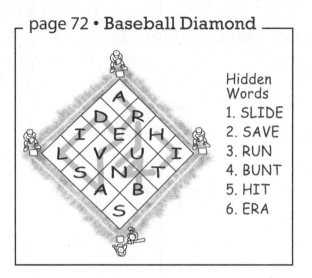

Hidden Words
1. SLIDE
2. SAVE
3. RUN
4. BUNT
5. HIT
6. ERA

page 103 • The "Whole World Series"

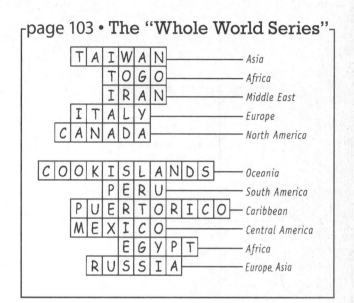

T A I W A N — Asia
T O G O — Africa
I R A N — Middle East
I T A L Y — Europe
C A N A D A — North America

C O O K I S L A N D S — Oceania
P E R U — South America
P U E R T O R I C O — Caribbean
M E X I C O — Central America
E G Y P T — Africa
R U S S I A — Europe, Asia

page 98 • How do you get …

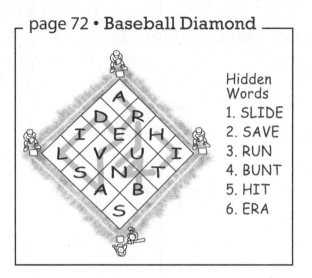

PLAY BALL!

GAME OVER!

PRACTICE, PRACTICE, PRACTICE!

page 91 • Game Pieces

fly ball

southpaw

home run

bullpen

page 107 • Name Change

BWLHACTKESOX

page 120 • Lucky Numbers

page 128 • How come Drew ...

~~AND~~	EVERY	~~CAT~~
TIME	~~GOT~~	HE
~~BAT~~	GETS	~~EAR~~
TO	~~FUR~~	THIRD
~~BUT~~	BASE	~~HIT~~
HE	~~HAT~~	GOES
~~HUT~~	HOME	~~BAG~~

page 124 • Secret Signals

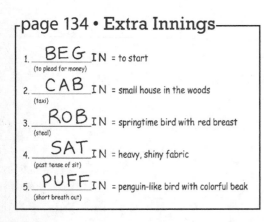

C A R E F U L — T H I S   G U Y

I S   A   P I N C H   H I T T E R !

page 134 • Extra Innings

1. **BEG** IN = to start
   (to plead for money)
2. **CAB** IN = small house in the woods
   (taxi)
3. **ROB** IN = springtime bird with red breast
   (steal)
4. **SAT** IN = heavy, shiny fabric
   (past tense of sit)
5. **PUFF** IN = penguin-like bird with colorful beak
   (short breath out)

page 137 • The Magic Number

The season has 162 scheduled games.			
	won	lost	games played so far: 152
TEAM A	93	59	
TEAM X	89	63	

Games TEAM X has won	89
ADD games TEAM X has left	+ 10
SUBTRACT games TEAM A has won	- 93
ADD the number 1	+ 1
THE MAGIC NUMBER	= 7

page 140 • ... Arctic Circle?

COLD
ONES

page 144 • Collectible Cards

HANK AARON
RIGHTFIELDER
ATLANTA BRAVES

HANK AARON
RIGHTFIELDER
ATLANTA BRAVES

page 143 • Dugout

1. UNI**F**ORM
2. G**L**OVE
3. PLA**Y**OFF
4. **S**LIDE
5. S**W**ING
6. F**A**N
7. BUN**T**
8. CA**T**CHER
9. ST**E**AL
10. **R**UN

1	2	3	4	5	6	7	8	9	10
F	L	Y	S	W	A	T	T	E	R

page 144 • Collectible Words

Possible answers to "Collectible Words": toll, bite, cell, bill, tile, belt, coil, bell, tell, till, toil, lilt

page 153 • Name Game

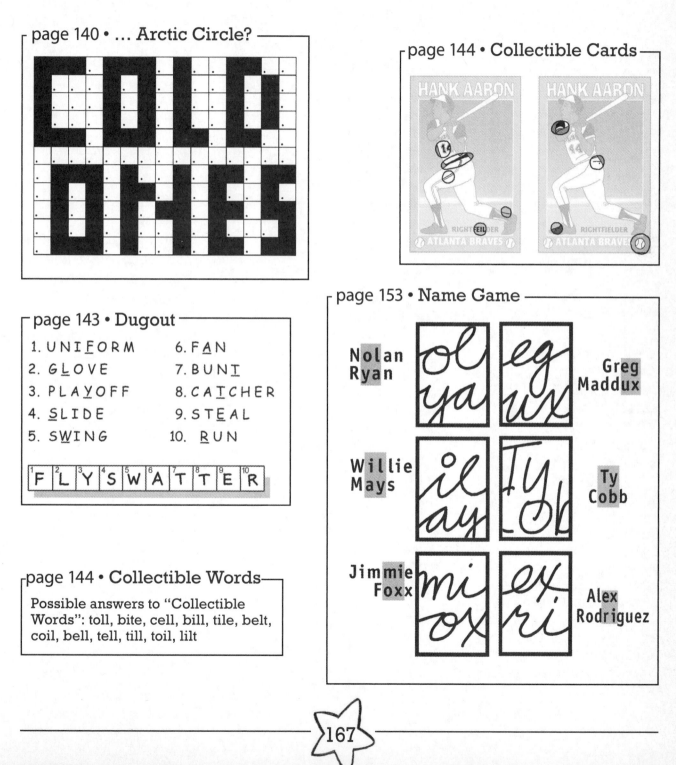

Nolan Ryan — ol ya

Greg Maddux — eg ux

Willie Mays — il ay

Ty Cobb — Ty ob

Jimmie Foxx — mi ox

Alex Rodriguez — ex ri

Index